The Gregorian Strategy for Multiple Deck Blackjack

The Gregorian Strategy for Multiple Deck Blackjack

Gregory Mannarino

LYLE STUART
Kensington Publishing Corp.
www.kensingtonbooks.com

LYLE STUART BOOKS are published by

Kensington Publishing Corp.
850 Third Avenue
New York, NY 10022

All Kensington titles, imprints, and distributed lines are available at special quantity discounts for bulk purchases for sales promotions, premiums, fund-raising, educational, or institutional use. Special book excerpts or customized printings can also be created to fit specific needs. For details, write or phone the office of the Kensington special sales manager: Kensington Publishing Corp., 850 Third Avenue, New York, NY 10022, attn: Special Sales Department, phone 1-800-221-2647.

Lyle Stuart is a trademark of Kensington Publishing Corp.

First printing: September 2003

10 9 8 7 6 5 4 3 2 1

Printed in the United States of America

ISBN 0-8184-0633-X

This book is dedicated to the casinos
What are you going to do now?

Contents

Preface

Before we begin, please allow me this moment. I would like to personally thank each and every one of the casinos of Las Vegas and Atlantic City for "allowing" me to live such an exciting and rewarding lifestyle. Even though you, the casinos, have at times made life a bit challenging for me, if it were not for you the Gregorian Strategy might never have come to be.

The development of the Gregorian Strategy is in fact a direct result of *need;* a need essentially created by you, the casinos. You see, you—and I am addressing you the powers-that-be in the casinos—were not content to just let me "play" as a card counter. Now, you casino bosses know very few of those individuals who can in fact count cards and know how to do it well enough to actually beat the game in the long term. I would conservatively estimate that one out of a thousand counters is in fact a true professional, maybe even less than that. A typical guy like myself can never hurt your business in any possible way, but still you barred me, shuffled up on me, forced me to play with heat, and just took the fun out of the game for me at that time. Well now, in retrospect, I am glad that you did, but at the time I certainly was not happy. You see, none of you had the foresight to think that maybe, one day, you would force a person like me to "rewrite" the game—and believe me, the Gregorian Strategy has now pushed this game to another level. I believe that this can be construed as a "Frankenstein effect": You created me.

With the introduction of the Gregorian Strategy, literally *anyone* can now beat the game, and beat it badly. Truth be told, I cannot wait to see what the casinos are going to do about this truly new and revolutionary strategy for playing the game of casino blackjack. The way I see it, you, the casinos, have essentially two choices. The first is, you simply leave the game alone and see what happens. As you already know, many of those individuals who read this book, regrettably, will not devote the time necessary to learn the Gregorian Strategy well enough actually to beat the game. But some definitely will, and there is no doubt that as the Gregorian Strategy catches on, the game of blackjack will not be as profitable for you as it has been in the past. Your second choice is to change the rules of the game. If you do that, you may end up costing yourselves even more money by alienating much of the blackjack playing public, because more people will avoid the game due to restrictive rules.

Why do many people play blackjack anyway? I will tell you. Generally, people have heard that the game of blackjack is in fact beatable, and this intrigues them. If the casinos do really change the rules of the game to such a degree as to make the game unbeatable, people will simply not play. People are not as unintelligent as you consider them to be.

So—and I am now addressing the Nevada casinos specifically—are you now going to bar players for simply using the Gregorian Strategy? I am sure that you can expect more than just a few lawsuits if you do that; eventually you are going to come across a judge who will deem it unlawful to bar anyone for simply possessing a higher level of skill playing one of your so-called games of chance, and then you may put yourselves in an even worse situation. Are you going to dictate which particular strategy people can use to play the game? I don't think so. It really is bad enough that, at the time of this writing, you are in fact allowed by law to bar anyone from playing *any* casino game if, again as you all claim, all of the games you offer are in actuality just games of chance. Now, we both know that this is not the case, don't we? I will see you in the casinos, and I assure you, I will be leaving with more money in my pockets than I came in with, thank you very much.

—Greg

As you my readers can see, I have no love for those who run the casinos, and there are many reasons for this. Believe me, I did not develop my bad attitude overnight. It took years. As you read through this book, you will find out why in more detail. But perhaps you and myself should now attempt to gain a little love for the casinos, because now you can also make a living off them. Just follow the advice that you will find throughout this book to the letter and learn the Gregorian Strategy as outlined in this book. You will do just fine. Let's begin!

The Gregorian Strategy for Multiple Deck Blackjack

Introduction

Welcome to the Gregorian Strategy

I was born in Brooklyn, New York, and, at the time of this writing, I am thirty-six years old. At this point in my life, I consider myself a true master of blackjack, *and there are very few of those in the world.* Throughout my years as a player of "the game," I have come across many people who considered themselves professional players. I can say in earnest that I have actually known only a few. A true professional blackjack player, before the advent and introduction of the Gregorian Strategy, was in fact an individual who counted cards. A card counter, *a professional card counter*, is an individual who possesses the skill to such a degree as to actually hold a long-term advantage over the game. This is very rare indeed. Personally, I have studied in great detail every known system for playing the game of blackjack, which includes every known counting system, including, for those of you in the know, everything from "Thorps ultimate," which I have mastered well enough to execute proficiently in actual casino play (not an easy thing to do, I might add), to the simplest unbalanced counts that are in vogue today. I have also studied, tested, and used in actual casino play every known betting system. These range from the real, which would be true count wagering, to the ridiculous, which would include every known progression-betting or progressive-betting system. I believe that I have taken this game to a level few before me have even achieved or imagined.

I am not a gambler in any sense of the word. In fact, I have never even bought a lottery ticket. To me, the game of blackjack seems like a viable investment opportunity. During my years as a professional card counter, and even more so today, I consider myself an *investor in the game*. Here we have a game in which the player can actually gain a mathematical advantage over the house if the game is "played" correctly. This is a very profound thing. What it means is that this game can provide a viable source of income for the determined player. You, yes you, now hold in your hand the goose that lays the golden eggs. You can do it; you can make it happen; you can actually make a living "playing a game." It sounds incredible, doesn't it? I am not going to lie to you: learning the Gregorian Strategy and executing it in actual casino play under fire will require a certain amount of work. But believe me, if you learn what I am trying to teach you throughout this book, the effort will pay back big. You are now my student. I have undertaken the writing of this book very seriously; it contains the culmination of my knowledge to date as a professional player, knowledge that can only come from experience, an invaluable asset.

I have completely dedicated the last few years of my life to creating a new, *modern* way for playing the game, the Gregorian Strategy. I can only hope that you are serious about becoming a winner. We shall see.

Later in this book, I will cover card counting and betting systems in some detail—which will include progression-betting systems simply for completeness—because, as you will learn as you read through this book, with the invention of the Gregorian Strategy everything that has come before is now moot.

The Making of a Strategy

From unassuming beginnings during my college years, going to Atlantic City to play the game just for fun and having no idea of what I was doing with regard to blackjack-playing strategies—that is, simply playing hunches or gut feelings—I moved on to wagering as much as a thousand dollars a hand as a professional card counter playing the high-stakes tables in the grandiose Las Vegas casinos. "The game" for me is in fact no longer a game at all.

I earned a bachelor of science degree from Wagner College on Staten Island in 1993. I then attended Bayley Seton Hospital P.A. (Physician Assistant) School and graduated in 1996. After having passed the national board exams with honors, I then practiced medicine at Staten Island University Hospital's main emergency department for the next three and a half years.

It was during my college years that I began to take up a serious interest in the game of blackjack. I learned that blackjack is not just another game of chance, but in actuality is a game of skill, with only *some* elements of chance involved. It was then that I became aware that it was actually possible for a skillful player to beat the game; so much so that certain individuals could essentially make a living at it! I became obsessed with the game at that point and bought anything and everything I could find relating to the game itself, its history, and its subsequent development throughout the years. Then I immersed myself in learning how to play the game to such a degree that I soon became a master of the old basic strategy and an expert card counter. This obviously did not happen overnight; it took hundreds of hours of study and practice at home before I tried my skills in the casino under fire.

Having then discovered the tremendous potential to make serious money while "playing a game," I often thought about playing professionally. What could be better than playing a game for a living? Making your own hours, answering to no one but yourself—you get the picture, don't you? Then, when I actually learned to play the game at the professional level—that is, being able to count down a deck of cards in twenty seconds with no mistakes—and after learning to alter my playing strategy in strict accordance with the count, I would go to Atlantic City every weekend to earn money playing "the game."

It was at that time I became acquainted with two other professional players who actually did count cards and were good enough to beat the game. Professional blackjack players can quickly and easily spot another professional. Well, I had been playing blackjack at Caesars Atlantic City for several hours when I was approached by a chubby gentleman wearing a baseball cap, (sorry if you are reading this, but you do look like that). He came over to me and asked me straight out if I was a professional player—a card counter, (but he obviously already knew the answer). I, having no idea who this guy was, quickly denied it, to which he responded, "You are full of s**t." He went on to tell me that he had been watching me play for a while and he was impressed. Then he told me his name and that he also was a professional. I still thought that he was working for the casino or something; I rarely trust people. *A word of advice here:* Be careful in the casinos—everyone has an angle of one type or another, trust me on this one. A few minutes later, a distinguished-looking older gentleman walked up to my new friend and me. It turned out that he was in fact a friend of my chubby pal in the baseball hat. The three of us went off to chat for a while. I still did not trust these guys at this point, so our little chat actually took place in the casino of Caesars Atlantic City. Well, it turned out that my two new friends had in fact been working together for many years doing what professional blackjack players do best—beating the casinos at their own game—and they wanted to form a "team" in order to maximize the return on their blackjack investments.

After some weeks and several lengthy discussions, we worked out the logistics and decided to form a blackjack team in an effort to capitalize on our chances at making some real money. The concept is very simple and effective. What we would do is pool our money, draw funds from that one combined bank, and then equally share the profits or losses. Playing this way, *as part of a team*, is almost like having an insurance policy and practically guarantees net profits at the end of the day. Here is how it works. Let's say you personally have a losing session, while your partners win; this offsets and absorbs your personal loss and offers a net overall win. This was a lot of fun, and we made a lot of money doing it. Each one of us would work a specific blackjack pit within the same casino. As we walked around the tables, we would "back-count"—also known as "Wonging," named after the master blackjack player and writer Stanford Wong. A Wonger stands behind the players and counts down the deck. Once it becomes favorable from a card counter's standpoint, the Wonger signals to his teammates to come over and play. Obviously, this was done as covertly as possible, and we would rotate casinos on a weekend, weekly, and sometimes even daily basis to keep our exposure to a minimum.

After we really got it down, we would average about four thousand dollars a weekend—split three ways, of course, after first taking a certain amount right off the top to increase our bank. This practice would allow us to increase our maximum bet spread and thus our potential for making more money. And make money we did, hand over fist, and we had a blast doing so. Here we were, really just three average Joes who were willing to put in a little time in order to be good at something, and we were actively beating the casinos at their own game! This "beating the casinos at their own game" thing was, and *is,* so exciting! Well, as we all know, all good things come to an end: the casinos of Atlantic City became aware of what we were doing, and playing became very difficult. Eventually, we split up and went our own ways. We had started our bank with a collective sum of nine thousand dollars. Two years later, playing usually only on weekends, we had accumulated nearly a hundred thousand! Well, I took my share and set my sights on the city of lights—*Las Vegas, baby!*

At that point in my life I felt confident enough, and I had become expert enough, to actually play the game full time. I left my lucrative job at the hospital to play blackjack *for a living!* This took a serious amount of guts—as a medical professional, I made a very good living. Still living in New York at the time, I would fly in to Las Vegas once or twice a month for a week or so at a time to "work." Playing at mostly $25-minimum tables, using a ten-unit spread—that is, going from $25 in bad counts to $250 a hand in high/good counts—and playing approximately ten hours a day, I would make about $400 a day, tax-free, or roughly $3,000 a week playing mostly double deck games. Well, after I did this for a while, the casinos of Las Vegas, as in Atlantic City, began to "get hip" to the situation. I was soon being shuffled up on (see Glossary) and sometimes asked to leave the casinos. This was a real disappointment for me, because I had worked so hard to become a professional card counter and player. Learning to play and count cards at the professional level is not easy, believe me.

Being forced, I began playing on the low-stake tables and cut my bet spread to five units in a futile attempt to keep playing and making money. Well, obviously I was not making the money I wanted anymore. Cutting my bet spread alone took a huge chunk of my advantage with it.

It was at that time that I began to analyze and ponder in great detail the differences among the blackjack games offered by the various casinos, the number of decks in play, the rules offered, and the then commonly used *old basic strategy*—which I knew, and every serious blackjack player knows (or should know), was *never* designed to be played against the most commonly offered casino blackjack games today, those with multiple decks.

As we know, the casinos hate card counters to the core; really, you must trust me on this one.

Now I had begun to bring together the basic idea, very basic at this point, that it may in fact be possible to beat this game by using a strategy alone—obviously *not* the currently-used *losing* basic strategy—with the current rules offered for multiple deck games.

Multiple deck blackjack games offer the player the most liberal rules—much better than those rules offered for single and even double deck games. Believe me, at this point I did not even have the slightest idea what I was really getting into! But looking back on it all, it truly has been worth the effort.

I began to work out my idea in extreme detail, playing out thousands and thousands of hands of blackjack, *one at a time*, comparing the use of old basic strategy against single deck games and multiple deck games while figuring out the mathematical probabilities for both. It became obvious very quickly to me that the differences are *extreme* with regard to probabilities, and it was again absolutely clear to me at that point that a new strategy was not only needed but *required* for anyone, serious player or not, still using the old basic strategy for playing the game. Again, at that time I still really had no idea what I was getting into. I began the laborious task of working out many more thousands of hands, *again*, one by one, and recording my results. I quickly realized that old basic strategy is more than just tragically flawed when played against blackjack with multiple decks (the most commonly offered blackjack game in the world). Believe me, it is no coincidence that the casinos have mostly all switched to multiple deck blackjack games. The powers-that-be in the casinos are not stupid. Here they offer to the public a blackjack game with multiple decks of cards in play, fully aware that players are still going to use a strategy, the old basic strategy, that was never designed to be played against blackjack games with multiple decks. It is like trying to mop a floor with a thumbtack. You need the right tool for the job.

You must understand right from the start that the old basic strategy was designed to be played against single deck games and single deck games only. Old basic strategy is actually just that, old—in fact, it is more than sixty years old. When this strategy was invented, the only blackjack game offered by any casino in the world was in fact a single deck game. Later on in this book, you will become more aware of the immense differences between games with one deck in play and those with more. Pay attention.

Now, after having become aware that the old basic strategy

is fatally flawed and contains many pitfalls when played against multiple deck blackjack, and after many long months of hard work going over and over plays and making corrections accordingly, I was able to work out the basis for the Gregorian Strategy. Still, even though I knew that this new strategy was true and correct from a mathematical and strategic standpoint, and as such should perform better, I did not yet know how much better. I then began to play out what would turn out to be tens of thousands of individual hands one at a time, *again*, and recording my results.

After an initial run of five thousand individual hands using the new Gregorian Strategy played out exactly as they would be played in a casino using common rules for the game—for example, dealer stands on soft 17, double after split, double on any two cards, no resplitting of aces, split aces only draw one card, and surrender—I was happy to learn that I was showing a 1 percent advantage over the house. I was happy, *but not yet convinced*, of the new Gregorian Strategy's true strategic power. Though five thousand hands may sound like a lot, it is not that many when you are out to prove that something works, especially over what is known as "the long run." I then ran off another ten thousand hands, again, played out one at a time by hand using common rules for the game, a truly time-consuming and mind-blowing process; and I was *yet again* showing a full 1 percent advantage. This is when I really began to get excited! Here I was playing nothing more than a strategy, as simple to learn as the old commonly played basic strategy—not counting, not ever changing my bets, using no "system" whatsoever—and after fifteen thousand individual hands played out by hand exactly as in a casino, not by a computer, I was astounded to learn that this new strategy actually did give me an advantage over the house! A full 1 percent, when played against multiple deck games with common Las Vegas Strip and Atlantic City rules. To reconfirm this, I played thousands of hands against the computer—and had the exact same outcome! I played the strategy against a card recirculating machine—many casinos are now offering these types of games—and still I was showing a distinct advantage. I played against a computer that shuffled the deck after every hand; still my advantage was there. I knew at this point I was on to something big, very big; *I knew that this new strategy could quite possibly be the biggest thing to happen to the game in more than sixty years!*

A lot of time had passed, probably a little more than two years—not to mention several thousand more practice hands—and now I was finally ready to try this new and truly remarkable strategy under fire in an actual casino. At this point, I had absolutely no reason whatsoever to believe that this new strategy would not perform exactly as it had in the controlled environment and against the computer. I was confident that I now had a true winning strategy! My excitement level was at an all-time high. I was ready.

I went back to it had all started, Atlantic City. I began playing at Caesars Palace. I remember the drive up that day, seeing the beautiful casinos all lit up from the Garden State Parkway, thinking, *I am back!* I pulled up to the valet, who very courteously took my car, and off I went straight for the casino. I must say, I truly love the casino environment; it is so electric! You have the beautiful atmosphere, the music, the lights, the action, the people, and the sound of coins coming out of the machines into the hoppers, *chang! chang! chang!* And hey, I am of the male persuasion, so I have to mention the scantily dressed cocktail waitresses. Also, the casinos on the weekends are hopping with action; there are people everywhere. It is a lot of fun!

So I sat down for the first time with my new strategy, knowing well that it was going to raise a few eyebrows, because generally, blackjack players who "think" that they know the correct plays will be quick to point out to you all of your "wrong" ones. Allow me to dispel a myth right here and now: Misinformed players, which is most of them, believe that if a player sitting at a blackjack table happens to play "badly," it "messes up" the game for the other players who "know how to play." *This is absolutely not true.* Think about it. Does it make any sense? As many times as you may think that a bad player hurts your play, that is how many times he helps you. Think about it again for a moment. The guy in front of you, the "bad player," decides for whatever reason to hit instead of stand, even though "the book" says otherwise. Is he in actuality pulling *your* card? Do you or do most players even have the faintest idea of what the probabilities are that he is in fact pulling "your card"? That card could just as easily have hurt you as it could have helped you. I will say this: if you are a card counter and the count is very high, and the guy in front of you hits when he "should" stand, pulling the "10" you were hoping for, that can really piss you off. But this is a case when the player—a professional card counter in this case—actually has a good idea of the composition of the remaining deck. It is in stark contrast to the average player who has absolutely no idea at all of the deck's composition.

So there I was in Atlantic City, my first time using this new strategy with real cash at stake. I was not crazy—trying out this strategy for the first time under fire, I was not going to play for high stakes, *yet*. So I sat down at a ten-dollar table to play. I sat at first base, the spot to the dealer's left next to the shoe, and bought in for two hundred dollars. The dealer began to deal and I recall him trying to "help me" several times because he did not understand my plays. He obviously had a fundamental knowledge of the old basic strategy and was trying to be helpful—which was nice of him—because he thought I just did not know how to play. Anyway, I soon was up a few hundred bucks and he stopped helping me. I subsequently went back day after day doing the same thing, and winning, without any problems from the pit bosses or other casino personnel.

Just another word of advice here. Once you study and master the Gregorian Strategy, *never* take anyone's advice on how to play a hand, unless of course he is also using the Gregorian Strategy and for a moment you are unsure of a particular play (at that point it would be prudent to stop playing altogether and review the strategy chart). Also, *never* give advice on how to play to anyone. If a player asks you what you would do in a particular instance, you can say, "I would do this," but then add, "but it is your money; you do what you want." The reason is that if the person takes your advice and subsequently loses, he may blame you. In my experience, I have seen arguments and even physical altercations in situations like this. Avoid it; you don't need the hassles. Also, if you keep giving advice to the other players at your table, you may draw unwanted attention from the pit bosses. I know, when you are good it is often hard to be humble; but in the casino, especially in Las Vegas, it would be prudent of you not to make yourself too noticeable. Got it? I hope so.

Now, for the most part, the casinos of Atlantic City offer a decent game, they are nice and fun to play in. In the summer you can take advantage of the boardwalk, which has all kinds of neat little stores, coffee shops, restaurants, nightclubs (for you party-a-holics), which are also plentiful within the casinos themselves, and of course the beaches.

The problem with Atlantic City, especially on the weekends, is the crowding. Often it is hard to even find a table to sit down and play blackjack, so there will be fewer opportunities to make money.

Well now, for me it was time to go back to Las Vegas. *I absolutely love Las Vegas!*

Las Vegas, Baby!

Currently I am living in New York again and "playing" in Atlantic City, which is only about an hour's commute for me; but I may well be moving back to what I truly consider one of the most beautiful and exciting places in the world—Vegas. Let me say this: if you have never been to Las Vegas or have not been there for a while, get there any way you can! Go by yourself, with your girlfriend or boyfriend, whomever, but get there. Stay out of the casinos until you have learned and mastered the Gregorian Strategy. Las Vegas, Nevada, is simply amazing; seeing it on TV does it no justice at all.The first time I went to Las Vegas was with my girlfriend; we were both totally blown away. We were staying at Bally's—which is an okay hotel-casino, but pales in comparison to some of the others, like the Bellagio across the street, the Venetian, the Aladdin, or Paris Las Vegas right next door, to name just a few. In fact, you can walk from Bally's casino straight through to Paris without ever going outside! How convenient, right? I told you, the casino builders and personnel are not stupid; they definitely do not want you to leave their casino, and they want your money, all of it, any way they can get it. Remember that! If you do happen to be in the casino at Bally's Las Vegas, bad boys and girls, you will see a corridor that leads to a lovely shopping area and buffet. Paris also has an excellent buffet, by the way; you must check it out. The casino itself at Paris is breathtaking in its decor and overwhelming in its scale, not to mention the exquisite exterior of the building itself. In the casino, the personnel wear little Parisian outfits; they even have "street performers" playing music, dancing, and performing. They spare no expense to entertain you in Las Vegas. The place is something else!

Strolling through the casino of Paris, you will simply be amazed. Walking out of the casino through the *huge* front doors, you will see a half-scale replica of the Eiffel Tower; the steel legs of this thing actually go through the ceiling and into the casino!

Continuing straight out of the casino itself, you will be standing right on Las Vegas Boulevard, arguably the most famous street in the world. To your left, you will be looking toward Mandalay Bay, a truly awesome casino adorned in gold in which you will find the famous House of Blues. The casino of Mandalay Bay is enormous. It is also one of the most beautiful in Las Vegas. If you go with the family or your friends, check out the "shark reef," a very cool aquarium-like place. Also, you must see the pool area; you will probably never see anything like it again. Next to Mandalay Bay, you will find the New York, New York, an astounding re-creation of the old Manhattan skyline. (Actually since the tragic September 11 incidents, it looks more like the new Manhattan skyline.) The casino in this place is massive, which means lots of opportunities to make money! If you walk through to the restaurant, you will come to another re-creation of old-time Manhattan, complete with cobblestone streets that feature actual steam coming up from the authentic New York–issue steel manhole covers. *Wow!* Across from that, you will find the biggest hotel *in the world*. The MGM Grand, adorned in magnificent emerald green, has fifty-five hundred rooms! And the casino is so immense, you can get lost in it. Good games can also be found here.

Where were we, now? Across from the MGM Grand is the Luxor, a modern rendition of ancient Egypt, complete with a Sphinx, obelisks, and other graven images—it is stunning. The exterior is entirely done in faux black onyx, complete with a Giza-sized pyramid. Inside, the elevators go up on angles to the guest rooms! If that is not enough, on top of this massive pyramid is the brightest light on Earth. It points straight up at the sky with a laserlike beam that's visible for miles and miles. In fact, on a clear night—of which there are many in Vegas—you can see the light from Los Angeles, California! Good blackjack games can also be found at the Luxor. Next door is Excalibur, looking like a medieval castle, complete with a moat—it is nice but kiddish, as is Circus Circus, down the Strip a bit. The only really good thing about either of these casinos is their blackjack games; both offer a good game with liberal rules. Actually, the Excalibur also has an excellent buffet. One more word about Excalibur: Go see the "Tournament of Kings" show.

If you ask me, the Tropicana has seen better days. Not only do they offer just a mediocre blackjack game, with restrictive rules, but the place is outdated.

The Bellagio is possibly the jewel of the Strip. Beauty and splendor abound; the place is understatedly magnificent! It stands on the site of the old Dunes Las Vegas. The Bellagio is truly a five-star showplace complete with dancing fountains. It also offers an excellent blackjack game, so keep this on your list of places to play. If you have the bankroll, go play in the high-limit back blackjack pit by the conservatory; it is rarely crowded, and they offer a two-deck game with outstanding rules. Another word: generally, the high-limit blackjack games offered by any casino put forward great rules; the casinos want to keep their high rollers happy. Across from the Bellagio is the Aladdin, a magnificent place with a very cool shopping area (if a bit over-priced) that is a nice place to stroll around. I cannot comment on its blackjack games because I have never actually played there. I have heard that they have liberal rules, though, and I am not surprised. The casinos of Las Vegas are in stiff competition with each other for your gaming dollar. They want to make you happy and comfortable.

At the time of this writing, Caesars Las Vegas is in the process of being redone with a life-size Roman coliseum being built that will sit almost on the corner of Las Vegas Boulevard and Fla-mingo. Caesars is also nice; the casino is beautiful, and the awe-some forum shops are worth checking out. The buffet at Caesars Las Vegas is overpriced and the food barely palatable, so avoid it. Decent games can be found there, though, so keep this place also on your play list. Across from Caesars Palace Las Vegas you will find a small place called the Barbary Coast. I am mentioning this place for two reasons. First, they offer a really good blackjack game with excellent rules. Second, this place has got to be the most paranoid about card counters in Las Vegas—more than you can possibly imagine.

Do you want to hear a funny story? You talked me into it. Back in my card-counting days, I used to bring my very attractive girlfriend to the casinos with me for a "counterattack" against the casino heat. If and when the casino pit bosses would give me "heat"—that is, bother me, stand next to me, or try to distract me—she would casually begin to flirt with them so that they would leave me alone. This worked every time, and she was great at it; us guys are such suckers for a hot girl! (Sorry, guys, I have to tell it like it is.) Well, this particular time playing at the Barbary Coast (I was living in Vegas at the time), I was in the back black-jack pit and the pit crew there knew me as a pro player (I knew you guys were not stupid, but I was just goofing with you). Soon four of the pit bosses came over, two flanking each side of the table; I must admit, you guys did make me a bit nervous. Well, my girlfriend—who was sitting right next to me and wearing a very low-cut, tight-fitting shirt—started saying, "It is getting hot in here" loudly, referring to "heat" and at the same time making a joke about it. She started pulling her shirt lower, with her fin-gers down the front, saying again, "Wow, it is really getting hot!" Just for good measure, she began licking the straw of her drink. Well, at this point, the four pit bosses who were there, as well as the dealer, were foaming at the mouth and could not possibly have cared any less about me. Anyway, I was up a few hundred at this point, so I just picked up my chips and we both walked away. She waved good-bye to them, and we laughed our way to the door. I have not gone back since, and I guess after this I will not go back for another long while, but we will see what happens. I do so enjoy doing things that may get me into some trouble.

Right next to the Barbary Coast is the Flamingo, the place made famous by the legend of Ben "Bugsy" Siegel. Sorry, Ben, but although this place is pretty to look at—especially at night, all lit up in pink neon—just keep walking right past. It has lousy blackjack games in comparison to the other places I have men-tioned, with regard to the liberality of the rules. If you like, you can stop in and have a drink at Bugsy's bar—they make good margaritas. Making a quick right coming out of the Flamingo, you will come up on Harrah's; this place is grossly overdone and noisy, but the blackjack games are good. Now making another right coming out of Harrah's, you will run into the Imperial Pal-ace—a cluttered, gaudy place, but its blackjack games are tops; you will want to play here. Down the Strip a bit and across the street is the Mirage, which is beautiful and offers a very good blackjack game—keep it on your play list. For one reason or another, the casino at The Mirage is always very crowded, so the best time to play here would be either very late or very early, depending on how you think about your personal clock.

Across from the Mirage is the Venetian, which in some ways is even more spectacular than the Bellagio. The Venetian actually has hand-painted ceilings; they remind me of Charlton Heston's classic movie *The Agony and the Ecstasy*. Where the Venetian now stands was once the Sands, of Rat Pack fame. Some of the magic of that bygone era still lingers on this sacred ground; you can feel it as you stand there. It is my understanding that in an attempt to discover where the famous "Copa" room actually was in relation to the current Venetian, the old floor plan from the Sands was laid over the new floor of the Venetian. It turned out that the old Copa room just happens to have been where the new main entrance of the Venetian is! Here you will also find good blackjack games with liberal rules.

Moving down the Strip a bit, across from the Venetian you will find Treasure Island. I love this place for its decor—and of course its excellent blackjack games with excellent rules. *You can make money here.* In this casino, you will find two-deck games that are dealt from a shoe. I am commenting on this only because this is the only casino I know of that uses this practice. Most two-deck games are hand-held games. Personally I prefer games dealt from a shoe, because there are fewer opportunities for dealers to manipulate the deck in an attempt to cheat the casinos, about which I really could not care less *(that's their problem)* and us, the players *(that's our concern)*. Believe me, dealer cheating goes on every day; more on this later. Are you still with me?

Continuing our trip down the Strip, you will find the Frontier, which is a cute little place but the blackjack games are lousy; no need to play here. Now we are coming up on the Stardust. Hi, Wayne! A nice place with excellent blackjack games and a great buffet; you will want to play here! *Please say hello to Carmen the pit boss for me.* Carmen, I am sorry, you were right about me but I could not tell you at the time. Please understand. I hope to see you again sometime.

Across from the Stardust is the Riviera, which also has excellent blackjack games; you will also want to play here. Did you see the movie *Three Thousand Miles to Graceland?* This was the casino in the movie. Farther down the Strip, you will run into the Sahara. Although outdated, it also has very good blackjack games.

By now we are almost in front of the Stratosphere. I love the Stratosphere. This place is truly unique looking and is probably the most recognized place in Las Vegas. The Stratosphere is the brainchild of Mr. Bob Stupak, a master poker player and businessman. I have never met the man, but I would like to. The casino offers excellent blackjack games; and if you get a chance, go to the observation deck—*what a view!* If you are feeling a little wild, try the "Big Shot," which is a ride on top of the Stratosphere tower. This ride will change your life. It is only for the strong of heart. I rode it and I thought I was going to *die!* Pretty cool ride, though.

Off the Strip a bit, you will find the Las Vegas Hilton, which at the time of this writing is for sale, if you have a few extra dollars and you are thinking of buying some prime Las Vegas real estate. The Las Vegas Hilton has one of the best blackjack games in town. Definitely put this place on your play list. When you walk into the casino through the main entrance, off to your right you will see a bronze statue of "the King." Go visit him. Also off the strip a bit is the Hard Rock Las Vegas. This is a nice place to visit but *do not play here!* At the time of this writing, the Hard Rock has possibly the worst multiple deck blackjack games in Las Vegas.

I must say something here. Casinos often change their rules for blackjack, and true to Las Vegas style, new casinos are always popping up. To keep current, you will have to go and check out the places for yourself.

Let's go downtown. The Fremont Street experience is something else. Down on Fremont Street, you can get a touch of what old Vegas was like. On Fremont Street and the immediate surrounding area you will find the Plaza, Main Street Station, the California, Lady Luck, the Golden Gate, the Las Vegas Club (more on this place later), the Golden Nugget, which is my favorite place downtown (hello, Harry), Binnions Horseshoe, the Four Queens, Fitzgerald's, and the Fremont (watch this place—I have been cheated here).

Most of the downtown casinos offer very good games. The best games downtown are at the Las Vegas Club, the Golden Nugget, and Main Street Station. If you must play single deck blackjack, among the few places that offer a decent game are Binnions Horseshoe, which is right within the Fremont Street experience; the Four Queens, also part of the Fremont Street experience; and the El Cortez hotel-casino, which is also on Fremont Street, but is off the beaten path a bit. If you live in Las Vegas, or if you are just visiting but have a car, I urge you to try some of the casinos that are away from the Strip. Most of the off-Strip casinos offer very good games.

Just a few more words on the Las Vegas area. Las Vegas, Nevada, is, at the time of this writing, growing exponentially. Actually, in recorded history, there has never been a faster-growing city. There are many opportunities for regular employment for those of you who do not want to play professional blackjack. Housing is amazingly cheap, and the taxes are very low. Nevadans, the locals, are also very friendly.

So there I was back in Las Vegas armed with a new, now totally proven strategy. Needless to say, it was the same thing there: no heat, no barring, and no worries; only more cash! In fact, you can make more money for time invested in Las Vegas than you can in Atlantic City, simply because you will find more games with better and more liberal rules. Later, we will go over the rules for the game one at a time. Pay attention.

I was then, and I still am winning with virtually no problems from casino personnel wherever and whenever I play. Only once did I get a remark from a pit boss, and that was recently playing in Atlantic City. He, the pit boss, really did not bother me, though; he only made a few comments about my strategy and the fact that I was winning. *Isn't it funny how they never bother talking to you when you are losing?*

Let's go back to Atlantic City for a moment. As I said earlier, you can find decent games in the casinos there, which means you can make money. The casinos of Atlantic City have all adopted similar rules with respect to their blackjack games, so jumping from casino to casino is less confusing than it is in Las Vegas; you know what to expect. Truth be told, Atlantic City does not even come close to the splendor of Las Vegas, but you *can* make money there, and that is what this book is all about. Throughout this book, I will make references to specific casinos, the games they offer, and other important facts. I urge you to pay attention to them.

The Gregorian Strategy Challenge

The Gregorian Strategy is the end result of tens of thousands of hours of intensive research and development, including computer analysis, thousands of individual hands played out in a controlled environment, as well as several hundred thousand more played out to date in actual casino play. You can rest assured that the strategy you are about to learn is "state-of-the-art"—a true combination of science, art, and strategy, which has not been equaled to date.

I am so confident in the Gregorian Strategy that I put forth this challenge to the advocates of *any* other strategy or system for multiple deck blackjack: *a showdown*, your system versus mine. We will play exactly as they do in the casino, using the most commonly offered game—a six- or eight-deck shoe with standard 70 percent penetration, dealer hits soft 17, double after split allowed, double on any two cards, split aces draw only one card, no resplitting aces, no double on blackjack. Ten hours of play, winner takes all. How about a card recirculating machine? I bet *not one* of the advocates of any other system will touch that one. But let me know. Get in touch with me through the publisher, and we will set it up.

The Gregorian Strategy is a marvel and is nothing short of a breakthrough based on pure science and applied strategy.

For far too long the casinos have held the upper hand by taking advantage of players using old basic strategy against games that the old strategy was never designed to attack. Now the tables have finally turned, and so will the game of blackjack as we know it.

Just to push this point home, think about this for a moment. In most casinos, you will find a gift shop, and most of them will sell you a pocket-sized chart that contains the old basic strategy. Believe me, if the casinos thought that anyone using the old basic strategy had even the slightest chance of beating the house due to a long-term advantage, they would not sell these charts.

Here's another very interesting thing to keep in mind: the casinos will even allow you to bring the old basic strategy chart to the tables so you can follow it to the letter. You are, in fact, allowed to bring charts or any other written aids to the tables. You are not allowed to bring calculators or computers to the tables, or even in the casino itself.

The Gregorian strategy is so revolutionary in its design and execution that it actually uses the casinos' own techniques, which once made the game more profitable for the casinos but now make the game profitable for you, the player. Virtually anyone who masters this strategy can actually make a living playing the game.

The key feature of the Gregorian Strategy—the one that makes it all work—is basically very simple: **By playing out your hands the mathematically correct way, using a strategy specifically designed to attack multiple deck games, and taking full** advantage of the rules offered as explained in this book, over the long run you will win at least 1 percent of all the money you invest into play.

Although you will not win a greater percentage of individual hands, with the ratio being approximately a 48 percent win for the player, you must remember that many hands dealt within the 48 percent will be hands you split, doubled down on, surrendered correctly, and took advantage of other rules offered as outlined later in this book, not to mention the fact that you get paid extra for your blackjacks. The dealer, although he will win the greater percentage of hands—approximately 52 percent—has to play out his hands also according to the rules; he cannot split, double down, or surrender, and does not get paid extra for his black-jacks.

Throughout this book, I will be attempting to explain the importance not only of being aware of the rules offered by the casino you may be playing in, but also of being fully knowledgeable about how to exploit these rules to their fullest, along with playing the Gregorian Strategy flawlessly, in order to gain your long-term advantage.

Playing multiple deck blackjack is *vastly different* from playing single deck. Old basic strategy was never designed or intended to be played against multiple deck games.

If you are new to the game of blackjack, I congratulate you, because you will be starting on the ground floor, learning a strategy that is revolutionary. As a new student of the game studying the Gregorian Strategy, you will be free from the biases that people build up after years of doing the same thing over and over again. I am referring to the millions, perhaps tens of millions of people who know and use an old, losing basic strategy for playing black-jack.

If you already know, love, and play blackjack, I congratulate you also. Although it will not be as easy for you to accept and implement the Gregorian Strategy, once you study it and, more importantly, understand its basic principles and application, you too will understand. It will be at this point that you will begin to reap the incredible rewards that can, *and will*, be yours. After learning the Gregorian Strategy, I urge you to not second-guess yourself, play hunches, or follow the advice of misinformed players. Learn this new strategy and execute it as I have put it down in this book and you will be a winner! You have already taken the first and possibly the most important step to playing a winning game: you were smart enough to buy this book. What you will get out of it is up to you.

Did you know that nine out of ten blackjack players have never even bought or read a book on this subject? So right now, simply the fact that you are reading this book puts you way out in front of most other blackjack players. You should be proud of yourself. Most blackjack players have simply learned how to play from someone else, who most likely had absolutely no idea of how to play this "game."

Human nature is interesting. Think about this for a moment. The average blackjack player is most likely a ten-dollar bettor; that is, he has no problem playing a ten-dollar hand of blackjack. That means that in one hour, at an average of one hundred hands per hour, the player in this case will have wagered a thousand dollars. Now, this average player can basically count on losing at a steady rate of 5 percent of each hand played. I am basing this rate on an "average player," by which I mean someone who has a basic understanding of old basic strategy and most likely will not make the correct play every time. So what am I getting at? This average player betting ten dollars per hand will lose fifty dollars an hour and has no problem doing that, but will not go out and buy a book on the subject in order to really learn how to play correctly. Also keep in mind that the average person does not even earn fifty dollars an hour at his job! You have just happened to stumble across what I consider the best book on blackjack written in the last fifty years! Do you see what I am getting at? The casinos are literally counting on the fact that 90 percent of their players will simply lose everything in a short amount of time. In a way this is good, because someone has to lose the money that we will win using the Gregorian Strategy!

♣ | 1 | ♦

The Game Today

With the development of the Gregorian Strategy, the game of blackjack can no longer be considered "just a game" by anyone who has mastered it. Implementing the Gregorian Strategy as outlined in this book has transformed "the game" into an enterprise, a moneymaking machine, not for the house (as in the past) but for you, and you *can do it*. The strategy you are about to learn will revolutionize the game of casino blackjack as we have known it for the last fifty years. For the first time *ever*, using a strategy alone, the average person can effectively beat the game. No special skill is required, no photographic memory, no genius mentality of any kind, just a little dedication that will pay for itself many times over.

Imagine being your own boss and answering to no one but yourself, able to do whatever you want whenever you want, "working" at your leisure. Imagine spending your time in multibillion-dollar hotel-casinos—not only making a living from them, but receiving comps, where they pay for your room, food, drinks, and entertainment! Imagine making your living playing a "game." Just visualize this: you are spending your summers in the sundrenched shore-lined casinos of Atlantic City, your winters in the casinos of the islands, your spring and fall with the lights and beauty that is Las Vegas. This is no lie, this is the life I have led, *and so can you* if you are so inclined. Yes, the life of a professional blackjack player is enviable indeed.

Since the beginning of casino gambling, sports betting, or, indeed, wagering money in any way, there have been those who have dreamed of making a living from gambling. Many, many have tried to play the game of blackjack for a living, and before the introduction of the Gregorian Strategy, only very few people in the world were successful in doing so over the long run. You hold in your hands the power to become one of the elite, not by the old ways, which involved complex card-counting practices, but by methods literally within your grasp right now. *It is up to you.*

What do we know about old basic strategy? It does not work! And will not work when played against multiple deck games, period. It is really that simple. You must understand that the old, commonly used basic strategy was never designed for or intended to be played against multiple deck blackjack games, the most commonly offered games of blackjack in the world today. The basic strategy is old, very old—more than sixty 60 years old, actually. Old basic strategy was invented when the only blackjack game offered by the casinos was a single deck game dealt out to the last card, with rules that you will not find offered today.

The funny thing is this: although the game of blackjack has changed dramatically with regard to the rules offered, the number of decks in play, and where the cut card is placed, the old basic strategy has remained basically the same. Throughout this book, you will learn specifically why the old basic strategy does not work when played against multiple deck games. You will learn why the Gregorian Strategy is the strategy of the future for the game of blackjack.

Unless you are a professional card counter, old basic strategy simply will not work from a moneymaking standpoint. A professional card counter often changes around his use of the basic strategy according to the count, along with using sophisticated betting techniques such as true-count wagering. Modern casinos are getting pretty sophisticated in their approach to detecting and subsequently barring professional card counters from play. Today, not only are casino personnel more adept at spotting counters, but the casinos are also using very high-tech software that actually analyzes your play from the "eye in the sky." If you are new to this game, the "eye in the sky" is the camera found above every game table that watches all the action in the casinos. I happen to know firsthand that the Golden Nugget in Las Vegas is using this type of technology. I don't mean to single out that one casino since I also know that most, if not all, of the big Strip casinos and even some of the smaller ones are using this type of technology, as well as *all* of the Atlantic City casinos. Eventually, the casinos will know that you are counting by the way you bet and modify your playing strategy according to the count. Always having to raise or lower your bet in direct proportion to your advantage or disadvantage brings unwanted attention to you.

Just for nostalgia, and for those of you who are curious about counting cards, allow me to briefly tell you how it works. First of all let me say this: *basic* card counting is so easy that it still amazes me how few people actually do it. And I am talking about people who consider themselves serious players. Anyone can do it; you do not need a photographic memory or stratospheric IQ to be a counter.

There is a mystique—or so people think—about card counting. Here is the "big secret" of how it works. As we know, a standard deck of cards contains fifty-two cards. We also know that a standard deck of cards contains four of each card: four 2s, four 3s, four 4s, four 5s, four 6s, four 7s, four 8s, four 9s, four 10s, four jacks, four queens, four kings, and four aces. Now, as the deck is played out during the game, the ratio of the cards with respect to each other is skewed. This "skewing" of the deck is very important to a counter. Why, you ask? Because there are times when a skewed deck gives a definite advantage to the player. When you know the deck is skewed in your favor, you have an advantage over the house and are favored to win; so to exploit this advantage you will raise your bet. If you know that the deck is skewed against you, you lower your bet to the table minimum. This raising and lowering of your bet is a dead giveaway that you are counting, *but it is the key to winning for a card counter*. It is a very simple and effective concept, but an eventual losing one because the next thing that will happen if you are in Las Vegas, and you are caught, is that you will feel a heavy hand on the back of your shoulder telling you to leave the casino, *or worse*. There are stories, some of them current, in which a player who was counting has actually been "back-roomed"—that is, taken to a back room and given a little "talking-to."

Recently, a professional card counter I personally know of turned up *dead*, gangland-execution-style, in Atlantic City. Many who knew him believe that his death was ordered by the powers-that-be, if you get my meaning. Let's get something straight right here and now: don't believe for a minute that there is no element of organized crime in today's gambling arenas. *Wherever there is power or money, you will find it.*

Okay, on to the basics of card counting. Arguably the most simple and effective count is called the high-low. There are many different counts, but this one is most commonly used. Each card of the deck is given a specific number. The 2, 3, 4, 5, and 6 are all counted as +1. If you see a 2 dealt, you would say, 1. If you see a 2, 3, and 4 dealt, you would say, 3. The 7, 8, and 9 are ignored—they are not counted. So if you saw a 2, 3, 4, and 9 dealt, your count would still be 3. The 10, jack, queen, king, and ace are all counted as −1. So if you are dealt a 2, which is +1, then a 10, which is −1, your count would be zero.

What does all this mean? If you know there are more high cards left in the deck, that would put the odds in your favor, and to exploit this advantage you would bet more. Conversely, if you know that there are more low cards left in the deck, you are a disadvantage and will subsequently bet less. A positive count is good, and a negative count is bad. This type of counting is called a "running count" and works with single deck games only.

If you are a card counter playing against multiple decks, you need to do a little more work. First of all, you must know how many decks are being used. As you become more experienced at this, you will be able to tell simply with a glance into either the shoe or discard tray. You need to take your running count and divide by the number of remaining decks to get the true count. *This is playing more at the professional level.* For example, if you have a running count of 10 and are playing a game using four decks with two remaining, you would divide the running count of 10 by 2 for a true count of 5. What this "true count" tells you is the running count *per deck.* Now, when you know the true count, you use it to determine how much to bet. Basically, you would bet half the true count in units. For example, if your opening unit is ten dollars, with a true count of 4, you would bet two units (or twenty dollars). That is known as true-count wagering, and it is the key to beating multiple deck blackjack games for a card counter.

That is card counting in a nutshell. That is all there is to it—no mystery, and no magic. Even if you are an expert card counter using old basic strategy, it is still very difficult to win. Believe me, I know, I am an expert counter who plays blackjack for a living. If anyone tells you different, he is a liar.

I can say this because it is true: I am an expert counter, and the system I once used was more complex and more efficacious than the high-low as described above. Now I exclusively use the Gregorian Strategy, so I don't have to count anymore. *No one does.* I even made it into the infamous Griffin Book, a more-or-less secret book kept by the casinos with photos of suspected card counters, card cheats, and others whom the casinos deem undesirables. Recently, the Maxim casino on Flamingo Road in Las Vegas closed down. Maxim was the home base for the Griffin Agency, the nice people who distribute the Griffin Book, and I hope that some of the agency's nice employees did not lose their jobs—what a pity that would be.

Yes, if you count cards, and you are good at it, you also can get into the book, and subsequently get barred from playing blackjack in Nevada, or worse. Today, learning how to card count is a total and complete waste of time. Does it work? Yes, but you will be learning a system that will eventually lead you to failure, because once you get good at it, the casinos of Nevada will not let you play. If you play in Atlantic City, the casinos are not allowed by law to prevent you from playing, but they will make it hard if not impossible for you to play or at least make any real money by shuffling up on you when you change your bet and harassing you.

All right, so we know about card counting, and as I said, it does work when used in conjunction with the old basic strategy, even against multiple deck games.

There are many types of counts—"balanced," "unbalanced," and others—but the one common factor among them is that they all *track the cards* in an attempt to find those times when the player holds the advantage. It is at those times that you the player, in order to exploit that advantage, will have to raise your bet, *and therein lies the system's downfall*—having to raise your bet. The practice of raising or lowering your bet is a dead give-away that you are counting. I could pick off a card counter in less than five minutes of his play, and so can the casinos—trust me on this one.

As you now know, the casinos hate card counters. They will hassle you, bar you, and even arrest you if you play in Las Vegas or Reno. Obviously, they cannot prove that you are actually counting, but they *can* arrest you for loitering or trespassing. I myself have had the Nevada trespass act actually read to me by a pit boss.

There are also many books written on blackjack that advocate the use of some type of betting system not related to card counting. These are known as progression- or progressive-betting systems. There are many types of progression-betting systems, not just for blackjack, but systems that are interchangeable from game to game. The simplest progression system—which is probably also the oldest—is known as the Martingale. If there were no table limits, *which there always are,* and you had an unlimited bankroll, this system would absolutely work. Here is how it works. The Martingale is a doubling-up-after-a loss type of progression that attempts to recover the original bet that was initially lost. The way the house beats this type of "strategy" is to impose table betting limits. Let's take a common table minimum and table limit spread. A five-dollar-minimum-bet table may have as high as a two-thousand-dollar-max. Never higher, most likely lower, but let's look at the extreme. First of all, you must remember that it is not at all uncommon to lose ten or more consecutive hands—this fact alone is the downfall of *all* progression-betting systems, not only the Martingale. Let's see what happens to a Martingale (doubling-up-after-a-loss type of progression) with ten losses.

In this scenario, the opening bet is only $5. You lose so you double up. The bet is now $10. You lose again, so again you double up, bet $20, lose, bet $40, lose, bet $80, lose, bet $160, lose, bet $320, lose, bet $640, lose, bet $1,280, lose . . . That is nine consecutive losses, *not at all unusual.* Your next bet, your tenth, if you were allowed to place it—*and you would not, because it would go over the table maximum*—would have been $2,560. All this is an attempt to recover the initially lost bet of $5. At the ninth loss, your total investment would have been the sum of your first bet combined with all of your subsequent bets in the attempt to recover the preceding bets, for a grand total of $2,555. This scenario was just a $5 one; imagine if it were a $10, $15, $25, or $100 one. You do the math.

There are more than several books on blackjack that contain multiple variations on betting progressions claimed to give you an advantage over the house. I don't want to spend too much time with this, but allow me to say: *there is no betting system, progression system or not, that alone will overcome the house advantage.* Period, the end, *believe it.* Real gamblers—who will eventually lose real big—use betting progressions. Any individual using a progression-type system, or authors of books advocating them, are hoping (*more like betting, and foolishly, I might add*) that probability theory will kick in and save them. Let me explain further. There is no "law of probability," it does not exist, there is only probability *theory*. There is, however, the *Law of Large Numbers*, which basically states that a trend that is continuing—consecutive losses, in this case—is just as likely to continue as it is to change. Thus, if you have just lost or won ten consecutive hands, that trend may well continue; the chances of its changing and of its remaining the same are identical. *That just about does it for the progression systems.*

Let's talk for a moment about the "Law of Averages." Yes, the Law of Averages does exist, but it will not help us when using a betting-progression system. Here is why. Let's use a coin as an example. As we know, a coin has two sides, so each time we flip it, in theory it has a 50 percent chance of landing on either side. What this means is that on "average," let's say out of one hundred flips, it will land on each side fifty times. If you actually do this in practice, you will see that it is just not so. Flip a coin one hundred times, and, more often than not, you find a distinct discrepancy between what you expect and what actually happens. Try it out for yourself. Often, of those one hundred flips, one side will be favored *drastically*. Now, let's say you flip that same coin one thousand times; you will then notice that the Law of Averages" is beginning to show itself. After one thousand flips, you will be more likely to find that the figure will "average out." It may take many thousands of flips of that coin to actually see the Law of Averages prove itself. Keep this also in mind when you are thinking of using some type of betting progression. Are you with me?

It is time for a *proven new strategy* that works without counting, without changing our bets, without changing our strategy, and *without a progressive-betting system*, all of which are doomed to failure. *This is the Gregorian Strategy.*

There are two ways to beat this game and two ways only. The old way is to learn how to count cards at the professional level and take your chances in the casino. The other, simpler, and *smarter* way is to learn the Gregorian Strategy.

This is the absolute truth: learning old basic strategy is a complete and utter waste of time if you plan to play blackjack in today's casinos; most of them only offer multiple deck games, as in Atlantic City or the island casinos. Even in grand old Las Vegas, many casinos are now offering only multiple deck games, or two-deck games with one deck cut off, or hand-held multiple deck games, or card recirculation devices such as "the King," and others. Just a word here on card recirculation devices. Personally, I do not trust them. I am not a very trusting person when it comes to gambling. People are ingenious, and I am sure that they can figure a way to make those machines work for them—the casino, that is. I am not sure how, but I am just about positive that they can, so be careful with these things, especially in smaller casinos off the beaten path.

The casinos are doing everything they can to make this game as profitable *for them* as they can. Well, that is all about to change with the advent of the Gregorian Strategy, and I just cannot wait to see what the casinos are going to do about it.

The reason casinos even use multiple deck games, or any of the games mentioned above, including card recirculating devices, is to give themselves even more of an advantage over the player using old basic strategy, card counting, progression betting, or any other systems.

The Gregorian Strategy is not a system; it is a strategy, a mathematically proven strategy that, when executed correctly according to this book, will give the player a distinct advantage over the house.

Card counters, users of old basic strategy, and progression bettors alike are paying at a distinct and profound disadvantage—even before the first card is dealt—against multiple deck blackjack games, and even single deck games with the rules commonly offered nowadays.

If you were lucky enough to find a single deck game with the same rules as multiple deck games (a game like this simply does not exist today), and you were to play perfect old basic strategy, yes, you would have an advantage of about 1 percent over the house. But those days are over. As a card counter, it is possible that you will play through many hands or even many whole shoes with low counts—you card counters out there know exactly what I am talking about—*that is, at a distinct disadvantage.* As such you are unable to make any money.

> *If you use the Gregorian Strategy, from the first dealt card through to the last, you will be playing at an advantage and as such are favored to win.*

Old basic strategy works, *more or less,* only with single deck games like they used to play back in the days when the dealer dealt out to the last card with rules you will not find offered on any single-deck game today. That is what it was designed for and those days are long gone, and so are the days of old basic strategy.

I have said this before, and I will probably repeat it several times throughout this book: playing multiple deck blackjack games or against card recirculating devices is *vastly* different from playing single deck. Let it sink in and believe it.

With multiple deck games, although the ratio of the cards with respect to each other remains the same, the total number of cards pooled together is larger. Now pay attention. What this means is that although the ratio of cards remains the same, your chances of pulling a particular card (for example, the all-important 10 or ace) are greatly reduced, and your chances of pulling a small card are greatly increased. In multiple deck blackjack games, then, you will be dealt a greater percentage of poor starting totals; your initial pair of cards is less likely to be a good hand. This puts you at an *immediate* disadvantage because you will have to "hit" in an attempt to get into the 17–21 range that greatly increases your chances of busting. Now, poor starting totals are not a problem for the dealer, because according to the rules of the game, you have to play out your hand first, and if you bust you lose, even if the dealer subsequently busts—a "technical" draw. Also, that 10 you were hoping for on your double down will be harder to catch.

Another very important reason the house likes to offer multiple deck games is that the dealer will make more hands *instead* of busting—that is, the dealer is more likely to beat you with a weak up card, thus once again increasing the house edge against you. *But* this works both ways: The dealer's chances of making a hand go up with multiple deck games, and obviously so do yours!

Second, since even our chances of busting also substantially go down with multiple deck games, those of us using the Gregorian Strategy will use this knowledge to *our* advantage and exploit it. The Gregorian Strategy for multiple deck games takes full advantage of these facts. Another thing to keep in mind is that with multiple deck games, because of the larger pool of cards you are being dealt from, your chances of getting a blackjack are reduced, thus denying you the 3:2 payoff. Are you starting to get the picture? This game is in fact quite complicated. I wonder if you have ever really thought about some of the things you are now learning. My guess is not, but I could be wrong. I don't think so, though. Are you paying attention? What am I going to do with you, anyway?

And so, I developed the Gregorian Strategy for myself. I never intended to share this new strategy with anyone but a select few, and as I sit here and write this I honestly do not know what possessed me to put this strategy down into book form. But I must say that it is exciting to think about how it will change the future of the game.

As a professional blackjack player, I used the old strategy for years, along with various card-counting systems, and did very well. That was until I got barred from playing blackjack in the casinos of Las Vegas because the casinos suspected I was counting, and they were right. That is specifically why I developed this strategy: as a result of need, just as I said in the beginning of this book, you will remember (or did you skip that part?). With a little effort on your part, you can make as much money as the world's best professional blackjack player, *without counting cards!* You will be able to play against any dealer using two or more decks, or even a "legitimate" card recirculating device (you already know how I feel about these things) using the strategy contained within the pages of this book under current Atlantic City or Las Vegas Strip rules, and you will still gain an advantage over the house. It is that simple.

Given the current rules offered for multiple deck blackjack, which are basically the same wherever we play, players using the Gregorian Strategy hold a mathematical advantage over the house!

I must make something very clear, *so pay attention boys and girls.* As you already know by now, the Gregorian Strategy is *specifically* designed to be played against games that contain two or more decks—multiple deck blackjack, the most commonly offered blackjack game in the world today. It is *not* designed to be played against single deck games, and it is recommended that you *do not* use the Gregorian Strategy if you are going to play single deck blackjack. The reason is this: As you know from reading the previous few pages, the Gregorian Strategy takes advantage of the fact that certain cards are more or less apt to be dealt out due to the larger pool of cards shuffled together. With single deck games, there are a whole new set of variables and probabilities. If you are going to play single deck exclusively, it is recommended that you use the old basic strategy. That is what the old strategy was designed for. Today, however, it is very difficult—if not impossible—to find a single deck game that offers all the good rules you commonly find in multiple deck games.

It is my honest, professional opinion that you should learn the Gregorian Strategy and play the types of games that it is designed to attack. You will do much better using the Gregorian Strategy against multiple deck blackjack games than if you learn the old strategy and play only single deck. If you do use the Gregorian Strategy against a single deck game, you will be placing yourself in the same situation as a player who is using old basic strategy against multiple deck games. The old basic strategy was designed to be played against single deck games, and the Gregorian Strategy is designed to be played against multiple deck games. You would not try to place a screw in a wall with a paper plate, would you? It is exactly the same thing here: you need the right tool for the job. Does any of this make sense to you? I hope so.

I suspect, unfortunately, that if more people start using the Gregorian Strategy, the casinos will eventually have to change the rules of multiple deck blackjack. Believe me, I love this game and do not want to see it changed around by the powers-that-be, especially given that it is how I make my living. But it really disgusts me that the casinos simply want and fully expect everyone to lose. Actually, it has always been a game of cat-and-mouse with the casinos and professional or even just proficient blackjack players. It is no secret that skilled card counters can beat the game—the casinos know this—but it is also a losing endeavor because of the hassles. Believe me, I have been there.

Let's go over a brief history of the game's development.

Before there was an old basic strategy, rules for blackjack were much better. At that time, even the house had no idea that there was a specific way to play that would give the players a better chance of winning. At that time, a "blackjack" paid 2:1 instead of 3:2 like today. You used to be able to double down on any number of cards, split as much as you like, or early surrender (early surrender is not offered by any casino in the world at the time of this writing). Early surrender allowed you to surrender as soon as the dealer had an ace up. Thus, if the dealer had a blackjack, you would not lose your whole bet, only half, by "surrendering." And, of course, all the games were single deck dealt out to the last card. Players and even the casinos themselves, including the powers-that-were at the time, did not know that there was a system of playing that would help the players win and minimize their losses. People playing the game had no idea how to make mathematically correct plays that would give them a better chance of winning and minimize their losses. People simply played on hunches, sometimes hitting hard 17 or 18 in an attempt to get to 21, even if the dealer had a 5 or 6 showing. (If you are new at this game, this is a horrible play and should never be done—although I personally have seen players make ridiculous plays like this one.) I believe that this says a lot about the nature of gamblers. Just think about it for a moment. When the casinos first introduced the game of blackjack, no one actually had any idea how to play the game, and yet people would flock to the blackjack tables and wager serious money on a game they had no idea how to play. It sounds strange, doesn't it? But it is true. The funny thing is, this still goes on today. People are strange, no doubt about it. But remember, the casinos are counting on "stupid players." These are the players they will welcome with open arms.

Then along came old basic strategy, invented by Cantery, Baldwin, Maisel, and McDermott, which of course was new then. This strategy revolutionized the game at that time, in much the way the Gregorian Strategy will today. The casinos panicked, thinking that their little game had turned on them, and got rid of all those good rules that we discussed on the previous pages (as you remember—or were you asleep again?).

Over the years, basic strategy underwent several subtle refinements, but it has remained basically the same even though the game itself has changed dramatically.

Then, in the 1960s, Dr. Edward O. Thorp, professor of mathematics and the "grandfather of card counting," came up with the idea of tracking or counting cards, to gain an advantage over the house. He released his book *Beat the Dealer*—and once again the casinos panicked. So much so this time that they immediately and drastically changed the rules of the game, convinced that all kinds of killer card counters were going to come into their casinos and take all their profits. This of course did not happen. But I will tell you this: if the people who bought Thorp's book had really read it, learned his system, and applied it, it certainly would have happened—especially in those days. In fact what did happen was this: the casinos in their panicked state changed the rules so dramatically that most players, not just the few who actually read and understood Thorp's book, simply stopped playing the game. This cost the casinos more money than if they had just left the game alone and let people play. You see, the powers-that-be really are not that swift. Well, after losing most of their action on the blackjack tables, the casinos reinstated most of the "prepanic" rules that were offered, and the game continued.

Dr. Thorp's principles were absolutely correct, and can even be applied today—except that there is no reason to work so hard anymore. Learn the Gregorian Strategy! Dr. Thorp, I hold you in the highest respect.

Thankfully, the game of blackjack is still evolving, *and therein lies the beauty of this game and what sets it apart from all other casino games.* As long as there remains the element of knowledgeable human input into playing a game—unlike with slot machines or games with bouncing balls or rolling dice, which really do have a fixed percentage against you no matter what you do, or, more importantly, what particular strategy you use—there will be ways to beat it! This is what so intrigues me about this game. Are you starting to understand that this "game" is really not a game at all, but an opportunity for a skilled individual to make money as an investment opportunity?

Using the Gregorian Strategy as outlined in this book, it will not be the house but you the player who holds the advantage!

Before we really begin, let's all get on the same page. What is the game of blackjack all about? Is it about getting to 21, as the name *21* suggests? No! It is about beating the dealer, plain and simple, and it is as serious as a heart attack because it involves money, a lot of money. In fact, the average blackjack table in Las Vegas or Atlantic City will win $250,000 a year from its players—and that is only one table! Every major casino has one or several "pits," or groups of tables, so we are talking about *serious* money.

Let's start right at the beginning. The game of blackjack is also known as 21, although the term *21* is becoming archaic, and rightly so. Calling the game *21* is misleading—and I suppose that is what the casinos wanted to do when the game was first offered, *mislead the players* in the hope that this would force players to lose their money more quickly. Calling the game *21* encourages the misinformed player to believe that he must achieve a combined card total of 21 in order to beat the dealer. Nothing could be further from the truth, and believe me, as you begin to play this game under fire in an actual casino with other players sitting at your table, you will begin to witness some truly unbelievable things with regard to the nonsensical "fly by the seat of your pants" strategy some people use. You will also watch them lose it all in a very short time. Do not feel bad for them. If they want to play like idiots, they deserve to lose. Besides, someone has to lose the money that you will win.

Today, blackjack is by far the most popular casino table game in the world, and the casinos make more money from their blackjack tables than from all their other table games. As a matter of fact, casinos win a staggering 6 percent of every dollar played! Sadly, this is coming from players using old basic strategy and using it against games that it was not designed to be played against. This is the truth. If you use old basic strategy, and play it flawlessly by the book, even against multiple decks, the casino will only have a small advantage over you.

If you find a blackjack game with good rules—which we will discuss later, so pay attention—the casino should have no more than a 0.5 percent long-run advantage over you, and this is *only* if you use the old basic strategy and play it strictly by the book. The reason the casinos win so much money from this particular game, even from players using old basic strategy that if played correctly only gives the casino a small advantage, is that most people do not even know the old basic strategy well enough. These people consistently make multiple mistakes, which cost them money and make the casinos rich—and the casinos love it!

Another mindless thing most people do is change the amount of money they bet from round to round. *This also adds to the casino's advantage.* Pay attention to this paragraph. There is simply and absolutely no reason whatsoever to change your bets either up or down unless you are counting cards. *No reason!* More than likely, these individuals, perhaps even you at some point, who are changing their bets from round to round have absolutely no idea whether the deck is good or bad—that is, rich in high cards or not (don't worry about it, it is a card-counting thing)—so most likely these individuals are raising their bets when they are at a disadvantage, and will usually lose. The house loves players like these. Are you one of them? Don't worry about it. Now it is your turn to get even.

When you learn and use the Gregorian Strategy, you will *never* change the amount of your bets. You will always bet the same amount, round after round. And you will win! In fact, when you play using the Gregorian Strategy, if you do change your bet either up or down, you will be putting yourself at a disadvantage. *Again, think about why:* you are not counting or tracking the cards and you do not have to! Playing the Gregorian Strategy alone will give you all the edge you need to consistently win playing blackjack. And herein lies another truly beautiful feature of the Gregorian Strategy: The casinos will never suspect you of anything! In fact, the casino personnel and other players are not going to understand your strategy because it is so different from the old basic strategy. Many of them will simply think you do not know how to play and may even make stupid comments to that effect. Let them. We shall see who laughs last . . . because it will be you who walks away with stacks of chips, and of course a big smug smile on your face! That is what I do.

If you do learn and use the Gregorian Strategy and play it flawlessly by this book, you will have a full 1 percent advantage over the house with common Atlantic City/Las Vegas Strip rules—and possibly more if you find a game with really liberal rules. This is a tremendous advantage!

What this means is that on average, you will win 1 percent of all the money you wager. Think of it this way: if you are playing head-on with a dealer at one hundred hands per hour, and twenty dollars a hand, on the average you will win twenty dollars cash per hour. That may be more than you make at your regular job!

Let me put this into perspective from a percentage stand-point. Playing the Gregorian Strategy, flawlessly by the book, overall you will win 48 percent of the hands you are dealt. You might say, "Well, if I am only winning 48 percent of the hands, and the house wins 52 percent, that does not make sense." It sure does! Here is why: although the house will still win more hands than you, even if you use the Gregorian Strategy and execute it perfectly, according to the rules of the game you can double down, soft double, split, double after split, surrender, and get paid extra for your blackjacks. The house can do none of these. This is why you must pay close attention to the sections of this book that outline the rules of the game and how to exploit them. Along with playing out your hands according to the Gregorian Strategy, this is how you will gain your advantage over the house. You must remember, it may take several hours or even several days for your edge to manifest itself. Even though you will have a definite advantage over the house using the Gregorian Strategy, you will not *always* win. Anything can and will happen in the short run. It is the long run that counts! Do you remember when we were talking about the Law of Averages? Or did you skip that part?

The next time you are in Las Vegas, Atlantic City, or any casino anywhere in the world for that matter, stop and look around you. Everything you see is built on small percentages that manifest themselves as time goes on. The casinos themselves do not win all the time—if they always won, people would not play at all. Even with games that have tremendous house advantages, like slot machines or keno where the advantage can be as high as 35 percent against the player, people sometimes win! Believe it or not.

With any kind of advantage, you will have your wins and your losses, with the wins prevailing. Your bankroll, which we will discuss later, will go up and down with an overall upward drift.

Take a look at the graph below. To the left, vertically, is your bank—this is your "bankroll," the money you have put aside to invest in the game, *not your grocery money, not your rent money*. On the bottom, horizontally, you have the factor of time. Looking at this graph, boys and girls, you will notice that now and then you experience dramatic changes in your bank as time and the game go on. So why am I telling you this? Because I urge you to pay strict attention to the money management section that is coming up later on in this book; this section often separates the men from the boys, or the women from the girls, or whatever.

A Random Walk With an Upward Drift

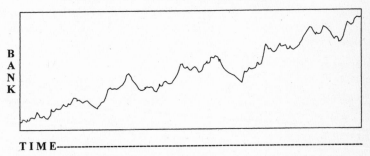

What about online gambling? I have had several people inquire about opportunities for making money using the Gregorian Strategy against blackjack games offered as part of the many Internet gambling sites available. I have very little experience with this type of gambling, and personally, *I do not trust it*. There are just too many ways in which a computer program can be manipulated to "cause" the house to win. I would say that if you just want to play for fun and take your chances, go right ahead. But if you are really serious about wanting to win, or you are seriously considering playing blackjack as a business venture, stick to the casinos where you can find *real* games and *real* opportunities to make some *real* money.

Just one more quick word on the subject of Internet gambling. A friend of mine, Trentino, has been using the Gregorian Strategy against one of these online gambling blackjack games and has done quite well. At the time of this writing, I have not calculated his win rate (although I should), but Trentino says he is doing well with it. That said, I still am not encouraging you to do the same thing. It is possible that at this point Trentino has just been lucky, and as I said earlier, personally I have limited experience with that type of blackjack game. For now, I will still recommend to you that you stick to the casinos for your blackjack moneymaking opportunities.

♦ | 2 | ♣

How to Play the Game

H ere is some more good news for you: wherever you play the game, be it in a typical Vegas or Atlantic City hotel-casino, a dust joint off the beaten path, on a cruise ship, or even at a "Vegas night" like the ones held by local charities, the basic play and layout of the game will be the same. *Please note, however, that I personally do not condone or respect a player using the Gregorian Strategy to make money from a Vegas night held for charity. Do me this favor: if you are in fact a proficient player and user of the Gregorian Strategy, save your skill for the casinos.*

If you have never played blackjack in an actual casino, it may not be a bad idea to get yourself into one to simply watch the action. Observe how the players interact with the dealer. Observe the speed of the average game, the shuffle, how the cards are dealt to the players, how the players place their bets and where. Note how the players tip the dealer, and how they interact with each other. Try to find a table that includes a new player coming into the game. See how he "buys in," observing the procedure the dealer goes through with a new player: how he lays out the money on the felt in a very specific way, and how he must call out to the pit boss in order to get permission to change a player's money into chips. Observe the dealer's hands, the player's hands. Observe a game in which a player is leaving the game, noting how the dealer will "color up" his chips. When a player "colors up," what is actually happening is the dealer will change the player's small-denomination chips into larger ones. For example, a player may have two hundred dollars in red chips, which are five-dollar chips. The dealer may color up to green, which are twenty-five-dollar chips. A player can also color up at any time, not just when he is leaving the game. Words of advice here. If you are in fact playing and winning, do not frequently color up your chips; this will bring unwanted attention to you from the pit and the eye in the sky. In fact, if you are winning, secretly place chips in your pocket on occasion. This is best done when the dealers are rotating their shift, which is usually every thirty minutes or so. To make this "chip hiding" a little easier for you, wear a jacket with large, easily accessible pockets that you can simply, and again with as little fanfare as possible, drop your chips into.

Another word about your chips. Let's say that you are on a vacation in a casino-resort or in a situation in which you will be spending a lot of time in one casino over several days. If you are winning, as well as hiding your chips, do not cash in all of your chips at the casino cage at the same time. If you are a winning player using any sort of strategy that can effectively beat the house at its own game, people will be watching you—trust me on this one. You never want to call a casino's attention to the fact that you are a winning player. There are many reasons for this, which I will discuss throughout the book, so pay close attention. These little tips are worth their weight in gold if you are going to have any longevity playing the game, especially in Las Vegas or Reno. Understand this right here and now. The casino personnel, with exception of the dealers and those not actually associated with running the game, *do not* want you to win. Oh yes, they will smile at you and they will be nice to you, but they need and want *all* your money. The dealers really *do* want you to win, because they want to tip them (more on this subject later). The dealers are thus actually on your side for the most part. The pit bosses, on the other hand, want and, yes, absolutely do need you to lose. Why, you ask? Their job depends on it, literally. Did you know that the pit bosses actually share in the profits of the games? Oh yes, this is true. And not just in blackjack. A pit boss can and will lose his job if the game is for some reason less profitable at the times he is working. Greed is the driving force behind those who run the casinos, pure and simple greed. Still, as Gordon Gekko said, greed is good! Now it is your turn: I want you to let greed be the driving force that will empower you to read through and learn from this book. This is your wake-up call, pal. You were smart enough to buy this book; let's see if you have what it takes to make it work. Let's start right here and right from the top. Time to put your thinking caps on again, boys and girls.

The game of blackjack is a card game; I hope that cleared up any confusion at this point. The cards themselves are numbered as follows: 2, 3, 4, 5, 6, 7, 8, 9, 10, jack, queen, king, and ace. Standard fifty-two-card decks are used. There are four of each card, each in a different suit, but the suit of the cards used in blackjack is irrelevant. A queen of hearts is equivalent to a queen of spades, and so on. The 10, jack, queen, and king all have an equal value: these cards are all valued as 10. The ace is counted two ways, as either 1 or 11. All the other cards are valued according to their numeric assessment—that is, a 2 is valued as 2, a 3 is valued as 3, and so on.

The game is played on a semicircular felt-covered table with the dealer on one side and the players on the other. There can be one to seven players. The seat to the dealer's extreme left is called "first base"—I don't know why, it just is. The seat to the dealer's extreme right is known as "third base" or the "anchor seat" and I don't know why, either. The term *anchor seat* is now archaic and rarely used except by some old-timers.

Incidentally, "anchor seat" does make more sense than "third base." Why, you ask? Because the player at "third base" is in fact the last player to play out his hand, so I suppose if in truth the third-base player is slow to decide how to play his hand, he can be misconstrued as slowing the game or "anchoring" it. I don't know, what do you think?

I must say something here. *Never* let anyone playing at your table, or even the dealer, rush your plays. Take your own sweet time making your playing decisions. If you rush, you may make mistakes—mistakes that will cost you money. Speed in your playing decisions will come with time, so don't rush it!

To the dealer's left is a device that holds the cards in multiple deck games; this is called the shoe. With one- or two-deck games, the dealer holds the cards in his hand, so there is no shoe. Actually, a few casinos do deal two-deck games from a shoe; Treasure Island on the Las Vegas Strip comes to mind. (While you are there, check out the free pirate ship battle show—very cool.)

To the dealer's right is a device called a discard tray; this is where cards already used in play are stored for the next shuffle. Just for general knowledge, it may look like the dealer is simply scooping up the cards and placing them in the discard tray haphazardly, but this is not so. The dealer picks up the cards in a very precise way and places them in the discard tray. Why, you ask? Good question! If there is a dispute between a player and the dealer, or even between two players, with regard to a payoff or the like, the dealer can actually place the cards back in front of the players precisely as they were dealt, so as to re-create the hands and settle the dispute. Cool, huh? Remember, nothing is left to chance in the casino; every action of the dealers and pit personnel is done for a very definite reason. You must take this "game" as seriously as they do in order to win—are you with me?

Now, when you sit down to play, the dealer will begin by shuffling the cards, and then he might offer you the plastic cut card. If you are playing one-on-one with the dealer, then you definitely will get the cut card.

Note: I do not recommend playing one-on-one with the dealer if you are new to the game. You may feel intimidated and/or uneasy, and may make mistakes that will cost you money.

When the dealer hands you the cut card, simply place it somewhere in the deck; it does not matter where. The dealer will then proceed to flip the deck to the opposite side of your cut card. He will then place the cut card somewhere in the deck—that is, he will cut off a certain percentage of the deck. *For card counters, where this card is placed is very important.* A card counter needs a game in which most of the cards are dealt out before the shuffle, also known as penetration. (Without getting too "deeply" into it, this is because a card count becomes more reliable toward the end of the deck.) Just for general knowledge, take notice as to where the cut card is placed by the dealer. You will see some dealers place the card deep, cutting off only a small portion of the cards, and other dealers place it shallow, thus cutting off a larger number of the cards. Okay, so why am I telling you this if it does not matter where the card is placed? Glad you asked, wise guy. This actually *does* matter in the sense that if the dealer places the card deep, cutting off only a small number of cards, you will be dealt more hands per hour and theoretically, because of your advantage using the Gregorian Strategy, you will win more! *So you thought you had me there, didn't you? You will have to get up pretty early in the morning to get me, tough guy, so watch yourself; I know where you live.*

Your other viable option would be to find a game that employs a card recirculation device. These things are showing up more and more—and why do you think that is? I will tell you, because, you see, I really do care about you, you know. The casinos hate "downtime" spent shuffling for the simple reason that it slows the game. The casinos know that most people are still using the old basic strategy, *at least at this point*, and will lose more to the house per hour if more hands are dealt. Also, the house likes to use these card recirculating devices because it renders card counting useless. Personally, I like a game that has *some* downtime for shuffling; it gives me a chance to take a break and relax. But you do what you want.

How much of the deck the dealer cuts does not matter with the Gregorian Strategy. The dealer could shuffle after every hand and it would not matter. You will still win!

After the dealer finishes shuffling the cards, he takes one card off the top of the deck and places it in the discard tray—this is known as the "burn card." It does not mean a thing; it is supposed to throw off card counters. *It does not work.* Simply ignore it. Just another quick little story here; as you are beginning to see, I love these little stories—and you should pay attention to them, because each has a lesson to teach.

I was playing at the Stardust in Las Vegas a while back, and having a meaningless conversation with a real knucklehead at my table about the cut card. He obviously did not know that I was a professional card counter at the time. So he went on to tell me that if the dealer did not "burn" the first card from the deck, he would be able to "count the cards." I wanted to laugh in his face—I did, actually. The cut card is meaningless to a card counter and even more meaningless to a practitioner of the Gregorian Strategy.

So now you are ready to play some casino blackjack. Accordingly, you will buy in, or place your money in front of you on the table felt so the dealer can change it into chips.

Note: Be careful. In Las Vegas, you are allowed to play with cash, so be sure not to place your buy-in money in the betting area (usually a circle or some other area marked in some fashion indicating where you will place your wager). If you do so, the dealer may think that you want to bet that amount on one hand instead of changing it into chips. I have seen this happen several times over the years. If you do not place your money in the betting area, it is considered "dead," and the dealer is not allowed to deal any cards to you. So place your buy-in money in a dead zone—next to the betting area, in front of the betting area, or behind it. The dealer will then change your cash into chips. As I said, you can play with cash in Las Vegas; but if you win, the dealer will pay you with chips.

By the way, the casinos use chips not only for convenience, but also to serve as a psychological attack against you. Later we will talk about some of the many things that a casino will do in order to more quickly and less painfully separate you from your hard-earned cash. When using chips, much like using a credit card, it does not actually seem like spending money, and people tend to be more cavalier about it. Did you ever think about that?

So the dealer has changed your cash into chips, and you are ready to play. Of course at this point, you have already read through this book several times, and have mastered the Gregorian Strategy so thoroughly that you can play it without thought. Right?

You now place your bet into the betting area, and the dealer will begin to deal from his left to his right, or clockwise.

With hand-held games, which contain only one or two decks, the cards are usually dealt facedown. You will pick up your cards with one hand and one hand only; never touch the cards with both hands. If you want another card, you will scrape your cards toward you on the felt table—but gently! If you do this in a rough fashion, you may bend the cards. And if you do bend a card, invariably the cards will have to be changed, which will slow down the game and aggravate the other players. Worse, the dealer and the pit boss may think you are trying to bend a card so as to "mark" it—as if to cheat. As you play this game in the casino environment, you are going to see a lot. Many people do indeed try to cheat by marking the cards by bending them like this, or nicking them with their fingernails, spilling things on them . . . just about every way you can possibly think of, and then some. Believe me, these people will get caught and dealt with accordingly; the casino is hip to all this nonsense. The moral of the story is, you do not want to be labeled as a cheater.

All right now, so you want another card and you have *gently* scraped the cards that you are holding in *one* of your hands toward you. The dealer will then give you a card *faceup* in front of your bet. If you go over 21—for example, if you had a total of 16 and the dealer gives you a 10—that would constitute a "bust," which is an automatic loss. At this point, you simply toss your cards—*gently again*—toward the dealer faceup. On the other hand, if you are satisfied with your total, you will gently slide your cards under your bet facedown. Remember, after you place your bet and the dealer begins to deal, do not touch your bet! The dealer may think you are cheating.

With shoe games, the cards are dealt faceup, and you *never* touch your cards with either hand. You will use hand gestures to make your play. Here is how it works:

- *If you want to hit, tap the table behind your bet.*
- *If you want to stand, wave your hand over your bet.*
- *If you want to surrender, simply say, "Surrender." (I will discuss this later.)*

With respect to the aforementioned games, my own favorite is a hand-held game. I feel more involved with the game; I like to hold the cards and play out my hands. Still, you find a game that you are comfortable with. It is important to feel comfortable as you play. If you do, you will relax and play more efficiently.

Just a word on blackjack dealers. Each has his own style. Some dealers seem to think they are in a race, and try to deal out as fast as possible. Actually, the dealers are instructed by the casinos to deal somewhat quickly, for two distinct reasons. First, the casino wants their dealers to deal out as many hands per hour as possible, to maximize their potential profits from the game. And second, the casino wants to force the players to make fast decisions with regard to their playing strategy in order to increase the players' chance of making a mistake. Do not let this happen to you. When it is your turn to make a playing decision, you just sit there and take your sweet time. The dealer cannot force you to play any faster than you are capable of, and he is not allowed to move past you until you make your playing decision. So, until you can play using the Gregorian Strategy quickly, avoid fast-dealing dealers. Got me?

You will want to seek out games with the most liberal rules; this will give you the opportunity to fully exploit the game so you can make more money faster, and that is what this is all about, right? The more liberal the rules, the greater the advantage becomes for you, the player, using the Gregorian Strategy. Finding games with the most liberal rules is very important; the better the rules, the more opportunities for making money. Remember that.

If I were to pick a particular casino either in Las Vegas or Atlantic City where I would want to play blackjack, it would be the Las Vegas Club at the corner of Main Street and Fremont Street in downtown Vegas—which, *in case you are hungry,* is right across the street from the Golden Gate casino. And the Golden Gate casino offers a $7.77 sixteen-ounce Porterhouse steak with all the trimmings that is to die for. If you do go over to the Golden Gate, tell Cookie, who happens to be one of the nicest pit bosses in Las Vegas, that Dr. Greg said hello. The Golden Gate is also the oldest casino in Las Vegas. By the way, the Las Vegas Club itself—the one with the excellent rules for blackjack—also has an excellent prime rib special. Check it out!

The Las Vegas Club advertises that it has the most liberal rules in the world, and it certainly does! Here you can surrender; you can double down on any number of cards; there are no limits on splitting, even aces; and you can draw as many cards as you want to split aces. I also should add that these rules are only offered on the club's six-deck shoe game, not on its double deck games—but that works out just fine for us!

If I had to pick an Atlantic City casino I would like to play blackjack in, it would be the Claridge—the only casino in town to offer surrender. If you are a high roller, upstairs at the Claridge in the high-limit area, they offer a four-deck game in which you are also allowed to resplit aces. I *really* hope that you are paying attention to these little things; this book is about making money. Are you with me?

I should also add that *all* of the blackjack games offered by every casino in Atlantic City are multiple deck games with four or more decks. The most common game offered in Atlantic City is an eight-deck shoe, no surrender, double on any two cards, no resplitting of aces, and split aces draw only one card. Dealer stands on soft 17.

If you were to compare Las Vegas to Atlantic City with respect to their blackjack games, *without a doubt* you will find better ones in Vegas.

Let's return to the theoretical advantage a player using the Gregorian Strategy will enjoy. Under the common Atlantic City rules for blackjack, the player will have a 1 percent advantage. In Las Vegas, with common Strip or downtown rules, the player will have just over a 1 percent advantage; the reason for this is the more liberal rules. In Las Vegas, a typical six- or eight-deck shoe game will offer all of the common Atlantic City rules along with surrender and resplit aces.

In Atlantic City, all of the casinos have adopted similar rules, but once in a while, just for kicks I guess, over the years they have been known to change them around a bit.

Vegas is a different story altogether. The rules are different from casino to casino, and they change with the number of decks used. It is very important that you know the rules before sitting down to play.

Do not play games with restrictive rules.

The key to beating this game is to play out your hands *strictly* according to the Gregorian Strategy that you will soon learn. Perhaps just as important is exploiting every last possible rule or anything else you can get—legally, of course. Later in this book, you will learn more about the importance of finding a game with the most liberal rules possible. Finding games with the best rules is an integral part of becoming a winning player.

As a general rule, multiple deck shoe games offer the best rules, and thus the best opportunities for making cash!

Ideally, the types of games that you want to play will offer—pay attention now—*surrender, double after splitting, doubling on any two cards, and resplitting of aces.* You also want to *try* to avoid games where the dealer must hit soft 17. If you cannot find a game that offers all of these rules and player options, *the essential ones are double down on any two cards and double after splitting.* You can work around the other ones, but you must remember, the less liberal the rules, the smaller your advantage will become. You can and will make money playing games with less liberal rules, but you will win at a slower rate. We are not in this game just for fun; *I sure know that I am not.* I don't know how anyone can have fun losing money. Are you *still* with me? I am beginning to worry about you.

Usually there is a card on the table explaining the rules; it is generally found near the discard tray. I know you already know where the discard tray can be found because you were paying close attention to the previous section—weren't you? Now, sometimes you will not find a card on the table so, if you do not, ask the dealer. It will usually state on the table's felt whether or not the dealer hits soft 17.

I cannot say this enough: knowing the rules is of paramount importance. You need to take full advantage of them so you can fully exploit your advantage. Let's go over the rules one by one so you understand them. Put your thinking caps on again right now and pay attention to the next sections.

The Rules

Doubling Down

To double down means that the house will allow you to double your bet and take only one more card—you will do this in very specific situations as outlined in the Gregorian Strategy. It is not important yet for you to know when specifically to make this play; you just need to understand how it works. To expand on this doubling-down rule, let's say you are dealt a two-card total of 11; the dealer is holding a 7 as his up card. Then the correct play in this situation is to double down. You will place a bet equal to your first *next* to your first bet, not on top of it, not in front of it, and not behind it, and the dealer will give you only one card. Now, why do you want to double down, you ask? Well, in this situation, the dealer is not in a very strong position, and you are. You are hoping to catch a 7, 8, 9, or 10, which—combined with your two-card total of 11—would put you in a very good position to win against a dealer with an up card of 7, and thus double your winnings.

Doubling down is a very important rule, and if you use it correctly, as suggested by the Gregorian Strategy, you will make money from it. You must take advantage of this rule as outlined later in the text. Pay attention.

Doubling Down After Splitting

If you are dealt a pair of cards that have the same value, 2,2 or 3,3 or 4,4, and so on, you will be given the option to split them into two separate and distinct hands and play them out accordingly. *This is also a very important rule.* You must split your paired cards correctly and in very specific situations so as to give yourself the greatest chance of winning. We will go over these plays soon. So, double after split means that after you split your pairs, you are again allowed to double down as described in the previous section. Are still you with me?

Resplitting of Aces

Most casinos allow you to draw only one card to each split ace. If you happen to catch another ace, you are stuck with a very poor hand. Some casinos allow you to resplit aces. Very few casinos will allow you to draw more than one card to each split ace. *This is not good,* but the Gregorian Strategy has some interesting recommendations when it comes to the splitting and re-splitting of aces, and we will go over the specifics soon. Read on . . .

Most casinos will allow you to resplit any other pairs of cards up to four times, except aces, and draw as many cards as you like to them. Let's say you are dealt a pair of 2s. According to the Gregorian Strategy, the correct play is to split. So you split them and the dealer gives you another 2—you can *and should* split again. If it is correct to split your initial pair, it is also correct to resplit and play out your hands accordingly. Again, it is essential that you do this correctly. Still paying attention?

Doubling Down on Any Two Cards

This is just what it says, for there are times when you will double down on a *soft hand*—one that contains an ace and another card. A soft hand is called "soft" because it can be counted two ways.

For example, an ace and a 7 are counted as a soft 18 because the ace is valued as a 1 or 11, plus the face value of the other card. So an ace and a 7 are an 18 or an 8. Soft hands, if played correctly, can make you money.

Never play a game that does not offer soft doubling!

Surrender

This is another good rule that will help you *lose less* when used correctly. To surrender means that the house will allow you to give up half your bet and get out of a potentially bad situation. For example, if you hold a two-card total of 16 versus the dealer's up card of 10, you will probably lose because the dealer is in a very strong position. In this situation, you will lose your entire bet approximately 70 percent of the time whether you hit or stand. Actually, if you hit, you have approximately a 2 percent better chance of winning than standing. Two percent is tremendous when we are talking about thousands of hands. If you tell the dealer, "Surrender," you will lose only half your bet. Hands that should be surrendered according to the Gregorian Strategy are a hard 15 versus dealer up cards of 9, 10, and ace; and a hard 16 versus 8, 9, 10, and ace.

If you are not allowed to surrender according to the rules, you *must* hit these hands against the aforementioned dealer up cards, until you either are in the 17–21 range or bust.

During your blackjack forays, you will see many people standing with stiff totals versus the dealer's strong up cards. You will also see them lose. Don't be just another loser like them; pay strict attention to and play according to the Gregorian Strategy no matter what your gut or other players may tell you.

Just to finish up on the subject of surrendering: it is the same as betting less in a bad situation, and losing it. It is better to lose half of your bet against strong dealer up cards all of the time than to lose your whole bet most of the time.

Dealer Hits Soft 17

This means just what it says. If the dealer hits soft 17, it gives the house a little more of an edge. Actually it is a very small edge, and really not enough to worry about. So if you encounter a game in which the dealer hits soft 17, as long as the other rules we discussed are permitted, sit down and play. Don't worry; you've still got them beat!

Insurance

If the dealer has an ace as his up card, he will ask if you want insurance. Insurance is in fact a side bet; in essence, you are betting on whether or not the dealer has a blackjack. Insurance costs you one half of your regular bet.

For example, if you bet ten dollars, insurance will cost you five dollars. If you take insurance, the bet pays 2:1 *if* in fact the dealer has a blackjack; otherwise you lose your insurance bet.

Insurance is a very bad bet. Never, ever take it, even if you have a pat hand, or even a blackjack yourself. Although sometimes you will lose, you will come out well ahead *in the long run* by not taking it. Trust me on this one.

Even Money

This is another very poor play designed by the house for the house. If you have a blackjack and the dealer has an ace up, he will ask you if you want even money. *Do not take it.* You will be losing out on the 3:2 payoff you get for your blackjack. The vast majority of the time, the dealer will not have a blackjack. You will make more money, a lot more over the long run, if you do not take even money, so don't do it!

I know that I am beating this subject to death, but I hope that you fully understand all that was contained within the last several pages. You absolutely must understand how the game works, and you must understand the importance of finding a game with the most liberal rules and know how to exploit them using the Gregorian Strategy.

Proper execution of the Gregorian Strategy will be described in detail throughout this book. Pay strict attention to the next chapter in particular. If you are unsure how the rules work at this point, I strongly urge you to reread the preceding pages. In fact, if you are a newcomer to the game, or even a seasoned "pro," why don't you go over the previous section just one more time? Go ahead, do it.

The Gregorian Theorem

This is quite possibly the most important section in this book; it is essential that you concentrate. You must completely understand the game and understand how and (especially) why the Gregorian Strategy works.

This chapter is intended to familiarize you with the basis of the Gregorian Strategy. Here I will attempt to describe for you, the reader and new student of the game, the foundation and fundamental principles of the Gregorian Strategy. You must develop a working knowledge that will allow you to fully understand and rationalize *how* and *why* the Gregorian Strategy recommends a particular play. This is very important. You must gain enough understanding of the Gregorian Strategy to know why you are making a play. If you understand why you are making a play, you will remember it.

Every strategic decision that you will make is based upon the dealer's up card, his potential for making a pat hand or busting with that particular up card, your initial two-card total, subsequent totals that result from hitting your hand, and your potential for beating the dealer's hand with that consequent total.

The chart below shows us the dealer's up card and his potential for making a pat hand (a hand in the 17–21 range) and busting with respect to multiple deck games.

This chart is in large part the basis for the Gregorian Strategy. Most people do not realize the dealer's pat/bust potential with multiple deck games. *It may surprise you.* To be straightforward, when I began my own in-depth studies into the game, I myself had barely an idea of the true dealer pat/bust potentials in multiple deck games.

Again, I want you to look at each component individually. I urge you not to just skim over it. Understanding this chart is essential as it will allow you to understand why we will make specific plays.

Dealer Up-Card Chart Demonstrating Pat Hand and Bust Potential for Multiple Deck Games

2 up, dealer will make a pat hand approximately 66% and bust approximately 34%

3 up, pat ~62%, bust ~38%

4 up, pat ~60%, bust ~40%

5 up, pat ~55%, bust ~45%

6 up, pat ~54%, bust ~46%

7 up, pat ~72%, bust ~28%

8 up, pat ~73%, bust ~27%

9 up, pat ~77%, bust ~23%

10 up (including J, Q, and K), pat ~ 78%, bust ~ 22%

Ace up, pat ~81%, bust ~ 19%

So what does this chart actually tell us? First and foremost, it clearly demonstrates that old basic strategy does not work, and will not work, when playing against multiple deck blackjack games. If you are familiar with the old basic strategy, I want you to think about the recommended plays, then look again at this chart. *This is why you have been losing!*

If you are *not* familiar with old basic strategy, either take my word for it or pick up one of the thousand or so books that advocate its use, look at it and its recommended plays—and you will see that it simply does not make sense. It really does not even give you a fair chance at winning when played against multiple deck games.

Second, the chart clearly shows us that with dealer up cards of 7 or above, we are in trouble. Going back to the card-counting theory for a moment, most counting systems consider the 7, 8, and 9 as neutral cards—cards that neither help you nor hurt you, or the dealer—*but as you can plainly see from the chart, these cards certainly do help the dealer.*

With a 7 or above as the dealer's up card, the dealer will make a pat hand between 70 and 80 percent of the time. Now, that is serious. Even with the 2 or 3 up, the dealer will make a pat hand more than 60 percent of the time!

Out of thirteen possible dealer up cards, that is the 2, 3, 4, 5, 6, 7, 8, 9, 10, J, Q, K, and ace, eight are bad: the 7, 8, 9, 10, J, Q, K, and ace. And only five are good, the 2, 3, 4, 5, and 6. To make matters worse, there are more of these dangerous cards in the deck—four each of the 7, 8, 9, 10, J, Q, K, and ace for a total of thirty-two bad cards, leaving us only twenty "good" ones. So again, out of every thirteen dealer up cards, eight on average will be in the 7-or-above range. Let's make this into a fraction, $8/13$.

What this means is that on average, the dealer will be in a strong position eight out of every thirteen hands—*that is pretty serious.* The next problem is, according to the rules of the game, we have to play out our hand first, so if we bust we lose, even if the dealer also subsequently busts, which is technically a draw. Actually at this point, doesn't it seem like a pretty unfair game? And for most players, it certainly is. The casinos love it, and the problem is *old basic strategy.*

Obviously, old basic strategy is not effective without card counting, and quite frankly, even with card counting it leaves much to be desired. A professional card counter, having some knowledge of the remaining cards left in the deck, will alter his playing strategy according to the count. For example, if you are a card counter and know you are playing in a game with a high count—meaning that there is a disproportionate number of high cards left in the deck—you may consider *not* hitting your stiff totals because the chances of pulling one of those high cards are now greatly increased. This altering of your playing strategy according to the count can be tricky, and in some instances may not actually be the correct play. We need a way to work a strategy, without card counting and without ever changing our bets, and still beat the house. Can it be done? It certainly can!

Look at the dealer up-card chart on the previous page for a moment—*and I really hope you are paying attention!* In order to gain and exploit your edge using the Gregorian Strategy, you know that you must take full advantage of the dealer when he is in the weakest position—with a 2, 3, 4, 5, 6, or (sometimes) 7 as his up card. How do you do this? You must take comprehensive and total advantage of the rules offered and subsequently double down against 2 through 7 when you have a hard 9, 10, or 11. Here is why. When you double down the hard 9, you will make a pat hand at least 53 percent of the time, and you will have twice the bet amount on the table. According to old basic strategy, you do not double a hard 9 against the 2 or 7, but according to the Gregorian Strategy, it is the correct play and it makes perfect sense.

When you double down on a hard 10, you will make a pat hand at least 60 percent of the time. Doubling down on a hard 11, you will make a pat hand 63 percent of the time, again with twice the money on the table. When the dealer has the up cards of 2, 3, 4, 5, 6, 7, 8, and 9, you double hard 10 and hard 11.

Overall—that is, over the long run—you *will win* most of your doubled-down bets. Again—*think about why*—you are taking advantage of the dealer when he is in a weak position and you are in a strong one and, as such, are favored to win! Pretty cool, huh?

You will no longer double down any cards against the dealer's up cards of 10 or ace.

According to old basic strategy, you are supposed to double down your two-card total of 11 against the 10 always, and the ace in single deck games. In single deck games, it is a good play, but with multiple deck games it is a loser. I see players making these plays all the time, and I also see them lose—and so will you. The dealer's up cards of 10 and ace are much too strong; if you do not catch a 10, you will most likely lose.

It may be time to take a little break, especially if you have been reading for a while. Let the information you are learning sink in. At this point, if you are unsure or do not clearly understand a particular section, go over it before you continue.

Are you ready to go back to work? Let's talk about soft hands. These are yet another way to get more money on the table when the dealer is vulnerable. As I explained before, a soft hand is a hand that contains an ace and another card, and as such it can be counted two ways. For example, an ace and a 6 are a soft 17, or a 7, because the ace can either be counted as 11 or 1.

Soft hands are overall the most commonly misplayed hands.

Actually the Gregorian Strategy is much simpler than the old basic strategy when it comes to soft-hand strategies. Are you with me?

All right, you know that you have to attack the dealer when he is in the most vulnerable position, so if you play your cards right—that is, double down correctly, soft double correctly, split correctly, take full advantage of the rest of the rules offered, and play out your hands properly according to the Gregorian Strategy—you have the potential to make money, and that is what this book is all about!

So what about soft doubling? You know that the dealer is reasonably strong with a 2 as the up card, so we will not soft double against the up card of 2. You also know that the dealer is strong with a 7, 8, 9, 10, and ace as the up card. So again, no soft doubling here. If you receive a soft hand when playing against any of these cards, that is the 2, 7, 8, 9, 10, or ace, you *must hit* it until you are in the 17-or-above range. In fact, if you hold a soft 17 (that is, ace/6), you must *always* try to improve it against *all* of the aforementioned cards. *Never, ever stand on a soft 17;* hit it until you either have a hard pat hand or bust. If you ever see anyone standing on a soft 17, you know you are looking at a loser.

If you hold a soft 18 (ace/7), you will stand against the 2, 7, 8, and ace. But again, you *must hit* your soft 18 against the dealer's up cards of 9 and 10. If you are not in the 19-or-above range when playing against the 9 or 10, you can consider yourself very lucky if you win. One more word on this "soft" 18: if you hold a soft 18 against the dealer's ace, my studies have shown it to be moot whether you stand with it or hit it and try to improve. That is, you will have the same chances of beating the dealer whether you hit or stand, so you decide what you want to do with this one. I would say stand, solely to avoid confusion.

You must understand that the average winning hand is 18.5. That's right, 18.5!

Now, I know what you are saying—"There is no such thing as a hand of 18.5"—and you are right. If you had the option of playing a blackjack game in which you were guaranteed to get an end total of 18 every time versus the dealer, *would you take it?* If you said yes, you would eventually lose everything. A winning hand is a 19, 20, 21, or blackjack. Believe it.

All right, let's regroup for a moment. The dealer is the most vulnerable with a 3, 4, 5, or 6 as the up card. These are the up cards that you will soft double against. When the dealer has a 3 as the up card, you double soft 17 and soft 18. When the dealer has a 4 as his up card, you will double soft 15, soft 16, soft 17, and soft 18. When the dealer has the 5 or 6 up, you double all soft hands up to and including soft 18.

You never double or hit soft 19 or soft 20. Instead, you stand.

What about hitting and standing decisions? When playing against multiple deck games, the old strategy has it all wrong. Let's look at the dealer up-card chart again for a moment.

It is an indisputable fact that with multiple deck games, the dealer will make a pat hand with a 2 as his up card approximately 66 percent of the time. Read that again, it is no typo: *66 percent of the time.*

With a 3 up, he will make a pat hand approximately 62 percent of the time! What this means is that if you do not have a pat hand yourself, you will lose against either of these cards more than 60 percent of the time! Old basic strategy recommends that for multiple deck games, you hit your hard 12 against either of these up cards. *This is fine*, but unless you are in the 17-or-above range, you can say good-bye to your money over 60 percent of the time!

First surprise. *You must hit your hard 12 against the dealer's up card of 2 until you have 16 or bust.* Look at the chart. What this means is, *you must hit your hard 15.*

I know this sounds a little strange to you old-timers using old basic strategy, but really think about it. Have you been winning using old basic strategy? I already know your answer.

With a 2 or 3 as the dealer's up card, the dealer will make a pat hand more than 60 percent of the time! I just had to say that again and I want you to really think about it. Pay attention.

When the dealer has a 3 up, you must hit your hard 12, 13, and 14, and you will stand on hard 15. Stop giving money to the casinos! Hitting your hard stiffs as above will put you into the 17–21 range more than 53 percent of the time in multiple deck blackjack games!

Remember, the dealer will make a pat hand more than 60 percent of the time with a 2 or 3 up. You must hit it, or you will lose!

When the dealer's up card is 4, it is a mathematical fact that, in multiple deck blackjack games, he will make a pat hand approximately 60 percent of the time. That is, he will bust only 40 percent of the time. *So you tell me: what will happen if you stand on a 12 or a 13?* Are you starting to "get the picture"? You *must* try to improve these hands. If you do not, and you follow the advice of the old basic strategy or other players who are just misinformed, you will lose. If you hold a hard 12 or 13, you must hit until you have 14 or above, or bust.

Lesson Number 2: never stand on a hard 12 or hard 13 against *any* dealer up card. That's right, *any,* including 5 and 6. Look again at the chart.

With a 5 or 6 up, the dealer will bust only 46 percent of the time! *That is less than half.* Most people do not realize this. If you hold a hard 12 or 13, again *you must try to improve it.* You will take one card, and then stand. If you do this, you will improve your hard 12, 71 percent of the time! You will also improve your hard 13, 64 percent of the time. Remember, one card on your hard 12 or 13 against a dealer up card of 5 or 6.

Just to drive this point home again, if you hit your hard 12, you will improve it 71 percent of the time! If you hit your hard 13, you will improve it 64 percent of the time!

Note: When I say "improve" with regard to the percentages shown, I am not saying that you will make a pat hand those specific percentages of the time. What I am saying is that you will end up with a higher total that may or may not be in the 17–21 range, giving you a better chance of winning the hand.

My studies have proven absolutely that these plays are mathematically accurate when it comes to multiple deck blackjack games. Yes, obviously you are taking a chance of busting the hand versus dealer up cards that are considered weak, but as you can unmistakably see on the dealer up-card chart, the dealer is never really that weak with *any* up card. Playing multiple deck games using the Gregorian Strategy, you will greatly improve your chances of winning by hitting rather than standing.

*   *   *

Let's turn now to pair splitting. There are some changes here also, and I will go over them play by play.

First, you no longer split aces against 10 or ace. With multiple deck games, the dealer is just in too strong a position with a 10 or ace up. Instead, you hit until you go pat or bust. Here is why—*pay attention*. Ninety-nine percent of casinos allow you to draw only one card to each split ace. This means that if the dealer has an ace or a 10 up, you only have *one chance* on each card to beat him when he is in a very strong position. If you hit your pair of aces, you will make a pat hand 79 percent of the time! Remember, this play is only recommended when playing against the 10 and ace. With all other dealer up cards, you always split. If in fact you are playing in a casino like the Las Vegas Club in downtown Vegas, which will allow you to draw as many cards as you like to your split aces, *yes*, by all means split them.

Next surprise. You no longer split 8s against dealer up cards of 9, 10, or ace. Instead, you surrender. If surrender is not available, you hit. *Splitting 8s is an overall losing situation when playing against dealer up cards of 9, 10, or ace.* You risk losing twice the money on a very bad play. Along with the 10 and ace, the 9 is also a very strong card for the dealer. As you know, the average winning hand is 18.5; all the dealer has to do is flip over a 10 and whack you. I honestly cannot believe that we (myself included in this one) made such a lousy play for so long.

When the dealer has a 4, 5, or 6 as his up card, you will split your pairs of 2s, 3s, 4s, 6s, 7s, 8s, 9s, and aces. It makes sense and it is mathematically correct; look at the chart. Then play them out as per the Gregorian Strategy as outlined.

When the dealer has a 2, 3, 4, 5, 6, or 7 as his up card, you will split your pairs of 7s, 8s, 9s, and aces.

Exception: Do not split 9s against a dealer's up card of 7. Instead, stand. The reason is that a vast majority of the time, you will already have the dealer beaten with your two-card total of

18. The dealer will likely have a 10 in the hole for a total of 17, so you will have him fair and square without doing a thing!

The Gregorian Strategy is designed to attack the dealer when he is the most vulnerable and take full advantage of the rules offered; this is where the strategy truly shines. When you are in a bad situation—that is, when you are at a disadvantage—the Gregorian Strategy is designed to make you lose less and overall win more by making the best plays.

All right now, here is where old basic strategy still applies. If you are stuck with a stiff hand, that is a hand of 12, 13, 14, 15, or 16, against dealer up cards of 7, 8, 9, 10, or ace, you must hit until you either bust or make a pat hand yourself, or surrender (see the Gregorian Strategy table for the specific hands that should be surrendered). Look at the dealer up-card chart again. You will see that the dealer will beat you a vast majority of the time if you stand with a stiff hand. Although you will lose most of your stiff hands by hitting, *you will lose less over the long run by hitting*. Many people have a problem understanding the "lose less" part, and I do not understand why. We are talking about small percentages, sometimes only a few tenths of a percentage point, but when we are also talking about thousands of hands, this small percentage can really hurt us.

For you hard-line believers in the old basic strategy, I know that it is often hard to teach an old dog new tricks, but let's look for a moment at each stiff hand and see what happens if you try to make it pat. Now, I know that some of you out there were just shaking your heads when I was talking about hitting your hard 12, 13, 14, and even 15 in some instances against "weak" dealer up cards. Again, refer back to the dealer up-card table, just to see how "weak" the dealer is, even with a 4, 5, or 6 up. Remember, we are talking about multiple deck blackjack here, and we are dealing with a completely different set of probabilities from those of single deck games.

Referring back to the dealer up-card chart again for a moment, you will notice that the dealer is not so weak after all even with a 5 or 6 up. Again, this is multiple deck Blackjack, not single deck, and it is to your advantage if you hit.

Here is what you can expect if you hit your stiff hands with respect to multiple deck blackjack games:

- *If you hit the hard 12 to pat or bust, you will go pat 53 percent of the time. This is very good.*
- *If you hit the hard 13 to pat or bust, you will go pat 45 percent of the time. This is still very good.*
- *If you hit the hard 14 to pat or bust, you will go pat 39 percent of the time. You will bust 61 percent of the time. Still not bad, and well worth the risk of hitting when playing against certain dealer up cards.*
- *If you hit the hard 15 to pat or bust, you will go pat 37 percent of the time, and bust 63 percent of the time.*
- *If you hit the hard 16 to pat or bust, you will go pat 36 percent of the time, and bust 64 percent of the time.*

You see, *you do not hit stiff hands if you do not have to*, but against specific dealer up cards, which include the 7 through ace, *you absolutely must hit!* Or, if the option is available, you can surrender (see the Gregorian Strategy chart). Again, you will lose less by hitting or surrendering.

We are just about there. Up until now, you have been learning how and, perhaps more importantly, *why* you will make definite and very specific plays according to the Gregorian Strategy. I hope you are not confused; if you are, simply go back and reread the sections that you do not understand. I strongly urge you to reread sections that may have confused you before you go forward. It is essential for you to understand why you will make the recommended plays according to the Gregorian Strategy. If you fully understand why you are making a particular play, you will remember it.

It may seem like common sense to you, but keep this in mind: just because you make the correct play, it does not guarantee that you will win that particular hand. Sometimes you will see the correct play lose ten times in a row. It does not matter; again, it is the long run that counts!

On the next page is a table that contains the Gregorian Strategy. The top line contains possible dealer up cards. On the left side is every possible combination of cards you will receive as your initial pair. In the middle of the chart, you will find the recommended plays. To use this table, you simply line up what the dealer has on top with what you have on the side. Use the key to see what the Gregorian Strategy recommends.

DEALER HAS

YOU HAVE	2	3	4	5	6	7	8	9	10	A
5–8	H	H	H	H	H	H	H	H	H	H
9	DD	DD	DD	DD	DD	DD	H	H	H	
10	DD	DD	DD	DD	DD	DD	DD	DD	H	H
11	DD	DD	DD	DD	DD	DD	DD	DD	H	H
12, 13	H	H	H	H	H	H	H	H	H	H
14	H	H	S	S	S	H	H	H	H	H
15	H	S	S	S	S	H	H	H, SR	H, SR	H, SR
16	S	S	S	S	S	H	H, SR	H, SR	H, SR	H, SR
17–21	S	S	S	S	S	S	S	S	S	S
A/2 or A/3	H	H	H	DD	DD	H	H	H	H	H
A/4 or A/5	H	H	DD	DD	DD	H	H	H	H	H
A/6	H	DD	DD	DD	DD	H		H H	H	H
A/7	H	DD	DD	DD	DD	S	S	H	H	H
A/8 or A/9	S	S	S	S	S	S	S	S	S	S
2/2 or 3/3	H	H	SP	SP	SP	H	H	H	H	H
4/4	H	H	SP	SP	SP	H	H	H	H	H
5/5	DD	DD	DD	DD	DD	DD	DD	DD	H	H
6/6	H	H	SP	SP	SP	H	H	H	H	H
7/7	SP	SP	SP	SP	SP	SP	H	H	H	H
8/8	SP	SP	SP	SP	SP	SP	SP	H, SR	H, SR	H, SR
9/9	SP	SP	SP	SP	SP	S	SP	SP	S	S
10/10	S	S	S	S	S	S	S	S	S	S
A/A	SP	SP	SP	SP	SP	SP	SP	SP	H	H

KEY: H = Hit   DD = Double Down   S = Stand   SP = Split   SR = Surrender

♥ | 4 | ♣

Putting the Plan Into Action

So now you know the theory and you have the strategy table. Now what? If you truly want to be successful, *you must practice and you must study*. In life, any worthwhile endeavor takes a certain amount of work. You get nothing for nothing. What you will actually pull out of this book in the way of becoming a knowledgeable and proficient practitioner of the Gregorian Strategy is in direct proportion to what you are willing to put into learning it. Do yourself this one favor: *until you know the Gregorian Strategy cold*, without thinking, so you can make the correct play every time, do not even set foot into a casino, let alone sit down at a blackjack table. It *will* undoubtedly take you several hours to several days, and possibly longer, to learn the Gregorian Strategy perfectly. Take your time and learn at your own pace. No one is rushing you, and I promise you that the casinos are not going anywhere. If you do prepare yourself correctly, it will pay big dividends. Prepare hastily and you have a recipe for disaster, in the form of having the casinos clean out your wallet for you. Please, you have come far in this book. If you learn from it and then apply it, *you will win*; you owe this to yourself.

I believe that the last few paragraphs are very noteworthy and need to be expanded on. Listen, no one likes to be lectured, but as a true student of the game you must take on this task of learning seriously. No one wants to see you become a winning player more than me; otherwise I would never have put the Gregorian Strategy down in book form. Believe me, I am already reaping the rewards of my hard work without this book ever being published. I just really want to see you, my students, win. Now, I obviously cannot force you to practice and study; ultimately it is up to you to bring it all together and make it work.

Believe me, I already know what *hopefully* very few of you will do—although unfortunately I do realize that it will probably be more of you than it should be—and what the casinos are banking on your doing. You are going to rush through this book and go hit the casinos like Chevy Chase in *National Lampoon's Vegas Vacation*. Forget it!

Here you have a true winning formula, and as I have said, it is up to you to make it work. So practice and study a little every day until you are ready.

Many studies pertaining to the art of learning have shown that studying a little each and every day, just before you go to bed, yields the best and quickest results. Study the Gregorian Strategy table; say the recommended plays out loud. Study with someone else; make up questions for each other. For example, ask questions like, "If the dealer has this up card and you have these cards, what would you do?" When you can answer all the questions correctly, or nearly correctly, and (very important) *understand why* you are making a particular play, then go out and buy yourself two decks of cards. Take the cards and shuffle them together. Then either by yourself or with a partner, deal yourself hands, play them out, and record your results. Doing this will help you build up confidence and prepare for actual casino play. If you are unsure about a particular play, refer back to the Gregorian Strategy table.

When you are finally ready to test your skills under fire in an actual casino, there are a few other things you need to keep in mind. Remember this, even before you set foot in the casino: *the casino is not your friend; in fact it is the enemy.* It sounds like a joke, but think about this, and *pay attention*, boys and girls.

First, the casino wants all of your money. They don't care who you are, or what your current situation is. They want you in and out of the game as fast as possible—broke, of course. Just in time for the next guy!

Second, the casino will do anything and everything within its power to stop you from winning.

One of the things a casino can and will do in an attempt to stop you from winning is try to distract you, with lights, noise, free drinks, and action.

Think about this for a moment: any casino will not only welcome, but welcome with open arms and big smiles anyone who consistently loses his hard-earned money to them. If the casino even thinks that there is a chance that you might win, as in the case of card counters or proficient users of old basic strategy, especially with single decks, they will not allow you to play.

Casinos claim that they only offer games of chance; skill (they say) plays no role whatsoever in whether you win or lose. This is true for all casino games except poker and blackjack. The casino will never bar any poker player from playing poker no matter how good he may be. The casino does not care, because the house always gets a certain fixed percentage of the pot. In essence, poker players are really playing not against the house but against the other players. In blackjack, however, the house feels that a skilled player is taking *its* profits because a blackjack player *is* playing against the house. So tell me, if blackjack is in fact only a game of chance, why then do the casinos have to bar anyone? Interesting, isn't it?

As of this writing, the casinos of Nevada are *legally* allowed to prevent anyone they wish from playing blackjack, for whatever reason.

In the casinos of Atlantic City, it is illegal for a casino to prevent anyone from playing blackjack. In a lawsuit that was won by a card counter, the late Ken Uston, the judge deemed it unlawful for a New Jersey casino to bar any player from playing blackjack simply because he possessed a higher level of skill than the average player.

I suppose the casinos of Nevada grease the right nuts, or did I mean to say "bolts"? If you get my drift! Are you still with me? Or are you daydreaming again?

All right, back to casino countermeasures. *The casino itself is designed in such a way as to make it hard for you to find an exit. There are no clocks, and no windows; you cannot tell if it is day or night.* I recall playing at the Sands in Atlantic City about a year ago. I was playing first base; at third base was a man literally falling asleep at the table. He asked me what time it was, and when I said, "Eight o'clock," he replied, "In the morning? Or at night?"

In the casino, even the cashier's cage is usually located out of clear view. The casinos go so far as this: *the rugs are deliberately designed to be hard to look at, in an effort to draw your line of sight upward toward the slot machines and table games.*

These are *just some* of the "passive" measures that casinos use in an attempt to "help you lose." However, they do have more direct ways of preventing you from winning. You already know about barring.

Let's talk about "heat." If you are playing blackjack and winning, many times a casino pit boss will come over and try to strike up a conversation with you in an attempt to distract you. Sometimes he may simply stand right next to you. This is especially true in the Atlantic City casinos such as Harrah's, Caesars, Resorts, the Hilton, and, the most notorious in my experience, is the Sands.

In Las Vegas, the worst casino for "heat" has got to be the Barbary Coast, which is on the corner of Flamingo and Las Vegas Boulevard. The second worst, in my opinion, is the Stardust. Sometimes if the pit bosses really suspect you of something, they will team up on you. That is, one pit boss will stand to your left, and one to your right. If they still don't know what you are doing, and they really want to make you nervous, a third or even fourth pit boss will come over. Boy, if I only had the time to tell you some of my war stories!

As I told you in Chapter One, during my days as a card counter, I would often bring along my very attractive and seductive girlfriend who would basically do the same thing to the pit bosses that they did to me: *distract them!* Another word on pit bosses: it is my experience that female pit bosses rarely give you heat—in fact, *very rarely*. In all of my years of playing, I was hassled by a female pit boss maybe twice.

Yet for all this, the most simple and *effective* "passive" way that the casino "helps you lose" is to *offer games with high minimum bets*. You see, the casinos know that 99 percent of the players are underfinanced, and they take full advantage of it. This brings us to the next chapter. Read on!

♦ 5 ♥

Money Management

This section is one of the most important in this book. Actually, it is probably *the most* important segment of this book! I strongly recommend that you not just skim through it. Money management is in every way just as important as the Gregorian Strategy itself, and it is an integral and critical part of being a winning player. If you are tired, do not read it now; you must pay attention to this section if you truly want to be a winning player. Money management often separates the men from the boys. Which one are you?

We shall see . . .

So what do you want to do with all your newly acquired knowledge? I believe that if you bought this book in the first place, *and you are still paying attention (which is pretty important),* chances are that you are serious about wanting to win. It is all in the attitude. You have to want it badly, like anything else in life that is of any worth.

When I first became a true student of "the game," I was extraordinarily focused and clearly determined to become a winning player. I wanted to be the best! I wanted to play blackjack for a living. I developed a clear picture in my mind, and I knew what I wanted. I was engrossed in getting there, and no one and nothing was going to get in my way. You now need to think about who you really are and what you are willing to achieve. What do you want to do with the information in this book? If you want to play blackjack for a living, enjoying the lifestyle you want and deserve, it is all here in this book—but ultimately it is up to you. If you are just tired of losing your money to the casinos during your weekend getaways to the blackjack tables, it is also all here. Everything you need to know about how to beat the game of blackjack over the long term is contained within these pages— everything. In reality, this is the last blackjack book you will ever need to buy. Are you the type of person who is really able to commit to something? Or will this book just become another decoration sitting in your house somewhere, gathering dust? Don't let this be the "fish that got away," so to speak. How many times in your life have you looked back on something and said to yourself, *You know, I really should have followed through with that; who knows what might have happened?* Well, here it is again. What will you do with it this time? So you were intrigued enough or smart enough to buy this book, or perhaps someone told you about it. In any event, you now hold in your hands a manual for making money. This book, if you apply yourself to it and actually do learn from it, will pay for itself multiple times over and may actually be the best investment you have ever made, an investment in yourself.

So who are you actually? Are you a recreational player who is just tired of giving your folding green to the casinos? Or are you an aspiring professional looking for a career change? I can tell you this: I play blackjack for a living, and as I mentioned in the beginning of this book, I once used the old basic strategy along with several different counting systems. My favorite was the Revere Statistical count. It is relatively simple and very effective. The life of a professional blackjack player is quite enviable, believe me. The freedom of being your own boss, being able to travel, take vacations, do whatever you want whenever you want is a beautiful thing. Then, as you know, my picture ended up in the Griffin Book and that was that. So what did I do? I am not a quitter. When I am determined to do something, it gets done. Period, the end. I was not then, and am not now willing to give up the lifestyle that I have worked so hard to achieve. As fate would have it, I have a very strong scientific background. I am also somewhat of a strategist. So I sat back, regrouped, and after a lot of hard work and a lot of time, I came up with the Gregorian Strategy. At this point, I am sure you will agree that it is quite extraordinary.

There are still several things that we must cover before you are ready to take on the mighty casinos and effectively beat them at their own game. Remember this, the casinos, Las Vegas and Atlantic City, were not built by giving away money; quite the contrary.

These magnificent multibillion-dollar cathedrals are raking in cash faster than the federal government, with yearly gross incomes higher than those of most countries. You now know only half the way to play a winning game. *Are you still with me?*

Personally, I don't believe that there is such a thing as a "recreational" blackjack player. It is not the nature of the game to be "recreational." Someone with an analytical mind, a problem solver, most commonly plays blackjack. *I also believe that no one finds recreation in losing.*

Now let's discuss your bankroll requirements. Yes, it is true, *you need money to make money.* That is just the way it is, and there is no way around it. Believe me, you cannot just walk into a casino with a hundred bucks and expect that you are not going to lose it all in a matter of minutes, regardless of anything else.

If you are a "recreational" player, then this section may not be very important to you. But I still strongly urge you to read it.

Let's regroup for a moment. You now have a proven winning strategy, one that will actually give you an advantage over the house. *Believe it.* But even if you were to play exactly as outlined it this book, *which is the only way you will have a chance at long-*

term winnings, this still does not guarantee that you will win. It means that you will *probably win.* Read on.

As we have discussed, the casinos make billions. *Billions!* given the small percentages involved, you must give the edge you obtain from using the Gregorian Strategy the time it requires to manifest itself. What it all boils down to is this: you must have a bankroll to play against that will carry you through the roller-coaster ride of blackjack. Is it possible that you will learn this new strategy, walk into a casino, start winning, and never lose? Sure it is, *but it is exceedingly unlikely.* You may walk into a casino and lose five sessions of blackjack in a row—does that mean you are doing something wrong? Maybe that is the time that you should reevaluate your play and make sure you are not making any re-peated errors. Making repeated errors of any kind using the Gre-gorian Strategy (*any* strategy, for that matter) will be enough to wipe out your advantage completely. This is for all intents and purposes why you must practice and study. If you make an occa-sional mistake, it is all right—we all do and we all will. Believe it or not, even I sometimes make a mistake once in a while. As long as the errors are not made on a recurring basis, they will balance themselves out.

Now, let's say you are playing perfect Gregorian Strategy in blackjack games with liberal rules, as outlined in previous sec-tions. What can you expect? *Long-term overall success.* You must, however, be prepared for the inevitable ups and downs of your bankroll. It is called *a random walk with an upward drift.* What this means is that, although your bankroll will eventually go up, it will not do so in a linear way; it will go up and down in a ran-dom fashion, but—as time goes on—will slowly creep upward. It works the same for the casinos, except they have a virtually un-limited bankroll. *The stock market works the same way,* and you "Wall Streeters" know what I am talking about.

In the real world, not too many of us have an unlimited bank-roll. So the true question is, How much do you need? I am glad you asked! You see, I knew you were not a dummy. To play at the professional level, *you will need four hundred times your bet as your bank.* Pay attention to this part! For example, if your bet will be ten dollars, you need a four-thousand-dollar bankroll. At this rate of play using the Gregorian Strategy, you will average ten to fifteen dollars per hour. With twice the bank, you will make twice the money, and so on. Remember, this is your bank, *your reserve.* You will never take your whole bank with you to the casino. Your bank will carry you through the inevitable swings, which are a natural and fundamental part of the game. My recommendation of four hundred times your bet is in actual fact a bare minimum. Stick to it.

The amount of money that you bring with you to the tables is known as your "playing stake." At the professional level, *this amount will be fifty times your bet, or one-eighth of your bank.* Again, this is a bare minimum. For example, if your bank is four thousand dollars, your bet should be no more than ten dollars. Your playing stake should be five hundred dollars.

I strongly—no, *very* strongly!—insist on your adhering to my recommendations for bankroll and playing stake if you are going to play blackjack at the professional level. Playing like this will prevent you from taking a major loss, and will allow you to rebound against your bank.

For you "recreational" players out there, you also should bring no more and no less than fifty times your bet, for the same reasons as previously stated. *Were you paying attention?*

What about playing multiple hands? You will often see players at the blackjack tables playing more than one hand; I recommend that *you* don't do it, and here is why. It is time for you to pay attention . . . thinking caps on again?

First, if you play multiple hands you will need a bigger bankroll and playing stake.

Second, a hot dealer can hurt you pretty fast.

Third, if you do play two or more hands, you must remember that you are really not doubling (or even increasing) your action and hence you will not double your win rate. The reason for this is called "linkage," in that your multiple hands are connected or "linked" to the dealer's one hand. Read on. Also, there is the "cancellation factor." That is, sometimes you will win one hand and lose the other; sometimes you will lose both, or win both, for a net win of zero. Overall you will win more, faster, playing one hand. Trust me on this one.

Players who do play multiple hands and use old basic strategy will simply lose money almost twice as fast. If you are a card counter, sometimes playing two hands or more is a good idea. This is, however, rare, for multiple reasons that I will not get into here because card counting is a thing of the past—*the Gregorian Strategy is the future of blackjack.*

If you want to win more, faster, seek out empty or nearly empty tables. You will receive more hands per hour and thus win faster.

For you aspiring pros out there—*yeah, you!* Listen, there is something else; it is called *discipline*, and if you don't have it, you'd better get it—*fast!*

Here is how it works. If you are playing on a table and you are losing hand after hand—for example, the dealer keeps pulling five- or six-card 21s—you had better get up and leave. Also, let's say you go to a casino and lose your playing stake. Don't rush off to the ATM for more money. Instead, sit back and reevaluate your play. Reread or go over the strategy chart. *You may well be making mistakes.*

Let me say something else. Dealers, believe it or not, have been known to cheat players, even in today's big modern casinos. I happen to know this *firsthand*. I admit that it is rare, but it certainly happens, with or without the casinos' knowledge. Most commonly, dealer cheating will take place in a game where the dealer holds the cards, as in a one- or two-deck game as commonly played in Las Vegas, but don't think for a minute that it does not happen in shoe games. I also have firsthand knowledge that dealers can and do manipulate shoe-type games. Have you ever seen what a professional can do with a set of cards? *It is amazing.* The truth is that this practice usually goes on without the casino knowing about it. Here is how it usually works. The dealer in question will have a person playing at his table who is "working" with him—the dealer, *not the casino*—in an attempt to skim money from the casino. The dealer in this case is a professional manipulator of cards, and he will manipulate the deck, or "stack the deck," in such a way that the person whom he (the dealer) wants to win always seems to get the blackjacks, winning all or most of his splits and double downs. At the end of the day, the dealer and his partner will split the cash they robbed not only from you, but from the casino also. In a real, nonfixed game, you might have gotten those cards the dealer saved for his partner. This practice is actually more common than most people think.

You will notice that I said "he," meaning "the dealer," throughout my little story. I did that on purpose. It has been my experience that female dealers very rarely cheat, especially young female dealers. So if you want to minimize your chances of being cheated, seek out games dealt by young female dealers. For those of you who prefer the fairer sex, don't let that cute female dealer distract you from your goal of making money. Play now and socialize later. Also *no alcohol* while playing. You really thought that this would be easy, didn't you? What am I going to do with you?

This is very important: *You must play out your hands like a machine.*

I am going to say this again loudly.

You must play out your hands . . . like a machine!

Never, ever play hunches and don't ever guess, because one mistake in twenty hands, one *repeated mistake,* is enough to totally wipe out your advantage. This is why you must know, learn, and play the Gregorian Strategy dead-on perfectly.

How much money do you want to win? Well, I suppose if you

were to ask me that question I would say, "All of it!" So should you! But be smart about it. Now, let's just say that you frequent a particular casino for a moment. Believe me, if the casino in question happens to notice that you consistently win more than you lose, you will get yourself into trouble, especially in Las Vegas. You must learn to limit your exposure in any one casino; spread it around a little. Never brag or tell casino pit bosses or dealers that you use the Gregorian Strategy. If casino personnel ever confront you about your strategy, you must make up some kind of a story. Tell them that you learned how to play from your friend, perhaps, but he, your friend, always loses and you usually do about the same. Tell them that you usually play each hand by how you feel at that particular moment. Never tell them that you actually bought a book on the subject of blackjack, *especially this one*. You must understand, the casino wants and fully expects you and everyone else to lose. The casinos hate, with a passion, a smart player. The casinos would be more than happy if all their players were drunk and stupid and had no idea how to play any of the games.

Here are a couple of rules that you must learn.

Rule Number 1

Never, ever—and I mean *never*—leave a winning table. If you are playing and doing well, just continue doing just what you are doing. Never put a limit on how much you can win.

Rule Number 2

If while playing at this lovely table, you notice that you begin to lose . . . it is time for you to leave the table!

With regard to Rules Number 1 and 2 above, there is something else that you must understand. It is called "biases." Biases are very real, and you must understand how they work because there is a way to make them work for you. *Paying attention, boys and girls? Thinking cap time again. Now place the cap squarely on your head—yes, right now—and turn it all the way up. Got me?*

When a deck or shoe is said to be biased, it means that although there is a random shuffle, the deck may favor either the player or the dealer. When the deck is biased in favor of the player, either the dealer keeps busting his hand or you, the player, keep getting strong end totals, a series of blackjacks, winning a bunch of splits and doubles, and *not* busting. The end result is a series of wins for you the player. *Players call this a lucky streak.* If the deck is biased toward the dealer, however, you may get into trouble. This means that the dealer keeps making his hands—pulling five- and six-card 21s or getting a series of blackjacks—or *you* keep busting your hands. The end result for you is consecutive or sustained losses. An illegally stacked or manipulated deck is an example of a deck that has been deliberately biased against the player.

The good news is, since you now know about player/dealer biases, you can use this new knowledge to your advantage. Here is how it works. Before you sit down to play, first observe the table. Watch the dealer through a series of ten hands; if he seems to be making most of his hands and the players are all losing, *stay away from that table.* I call this type of table a "negatively biased table." On the other hand, if you observe that the dealer is busting more than usual and the players are winning, just sit down and play: you have found a table with a "positive bias."

Each and every time I play, I first walk around the blackjack pits observing the games, looking for a positively biased table. I strongly urge you to do the same if you are to maximize your winnings.

Understanding biases is very significant. You will see many players just sitting there at the blackjack table losing hand after hand, foolishly saying out loud, "The cards are going to come around," or "my luck has to change sometime, I can't lose every hand." *Wrong.* Remember when we were talking about the *Law of Large Numbers?* Or did you skip that part! Understanding biases is an integral part of being a winning player. Are you a winner? Or just another loser? *We shall soon see.* Some may argue that if in fact a deck is biased either positively or negatively, and then another player, *perhaps you*, comes and sits down to play, that bias is likely to change. To those people I would say, "Hogwash!" I would be willing to bet, *no pun intended,* that I personally have spent more time studying, understanding, and actually playing this game than most other people on this planet. I can tell you from my personal experience that this argument about a bias changing is *highly unlikely.*

More good news about biases: it has also been my experience that the more decks are used in play, the longer the bias will last. *This is important.* Sometimes, probably more often than not, if you find a multiple deck game—I am specifically talking about four or more decks with a positive bias—even after the shuffle, that same set of cards tends to keep that positive bias. This goes back to Rule Number 1—never leave a winning table. Many casinos use a shuffling machine in which there are two distinct decks of cards. These two packs will usually have different-colored backs—for example, red and blue. The reason casinos use shuffling machines with two distinct decks is to keep the game going. The casinos hate downtime taken for shuffling because it costs them money, so as one deck is being dealt to the players, the other is being shuffled. Why am I telling you this? Well, pay attention to the differences between the two decks. For example, the red one may have a positive bias and the blue one may have a negative bias. You will want to leave the table when the negatively biased deck is dealt, and subsequently return when the deck that had the positive bias returns to play. Another secret: *the casinos also know about biases,* believe me. They don't advertise it, but they surely know. So what do the casinos do to counteract these biases? Every couple of hours, among the several other reasons for doing this, they change the cards. This can be a real disappointment, but let's say you happen to come across a positively biased deck and are doing well. Don't be afraid to ask the pit boss to let the dealer deal out another shoe before he changes decks. But don't just come out and say, "Hey Mr. Pit Boss, I have a positively biased deck here, and I don't want to see it go." Just say, "Can you *please* wait for one more shoe? We are all doing so well *for a change"*—add that you just lost your shirt an hour ago playing at the craps table and you are only now winning some back *(you have to learn to lie a little)*—"and we are afraid that a new deck will mess it up." You must play dumb; the casinos really don't want to give away any money at all, and they hate smart players. You need to do anything and everything—*legally, of course*—to maximize your winnings.

The reason you are reading this book is because you want to be a winner, right? It is up to you to make it work. I would say that more than 98 percent of all blackjack players have absolutely no idea of how to play this "game." Believe me, this is not a game at all—playing blackjack can be as lucrative as you want it to be. Listen to me, ye of little faith.

Learn to keep a record of your play. I suggest that you keep a small notebook, one that you can stash in your pocket. In it you should write *where you played, the rules offered at the time, buy in, bet size, win/loss, heat, and time of day.* This is important, as it will allow you to track your development. Do not allow any of the casino personnel see you keeping a record of your play because only a professional would do this type of thing, and casinos hate professionals. This record keeping is also good thing because by keeping a record of your play, you will be able to track your progress over time. Also, if you do get heat from casino personnel, you will have recorded where and when so you can avoid that blackjack pit for a while, or even the entire casino for a while. Remember, play smart!

♥ | 6 | ♦

Casino Etiquette

Certain types of behavior are expected and are often encouraged within the casino environment. For the newcomer to the casinos, the atmosphere alone can be somewhat overwhelming. You must keep in mind at all times that nothing is left to chance by the casino. As soon as you set foot in the casino, the atmosphere, the lights, the action, the setup (where the slot machines are in relation to the table games), the temperature, the rugs, *everything*, is specifically designed with one thing in mind: to separate you from your cash. Period; remember that. You must be aware of these things if you are to become a winning player.

Depending on which game you play, you will have to alter your personality to fit it. The loudest game in the casino is craps; you can usually hear a craps game across the street from the casino. Okay, I am exaggerating here, but actually they can be loud at times. Most other casino games are more reserved, for several reasons. But back to blackjack.

Blackjack players generally do not yell out either after a win or a loss. They are more reserved, quiet. Crying out is not encouraged when playing this game, as it is in a game of craps. Blackjack is unique in that each player is more or less in his own little environment, distinct from the rest of the casino action. Let's look at an example: first of all, the casino makes sure you are seated comfortably, in your own little betting area—unlike any other casino table game, where people often share betting areas. You relate to the dealer on an individual basis. You make your own playing decisions, *right or wrong*, and you alone are responsible for their outcomes. This uniqueness to the game, although beneficial to the knowledgeable player, can actually hurt the average player and cost him money. The reason is that this little private environment, along with all the other casino ploys to separate you from your money, exerts yet another psychological effect: it can make you feel helpless if you are losing. So what do people in this helpless state do? Since they feel helpless anyway, they just sit there until they lose it all. You will see many players without any discipline or even the most basic knowledge of the game sitting as if in a trance, simply "giving" their money to the casinos, and the casinos very happily obliging.

So is it all right to be happy if you just won a few hundred bucks on a hand on which you split and doubled several times? Absolutely! At a time like this, it is also customary to tip the dealer. Tipping is customary if you receive several good hands in a row, too, or two blackjacks back to back.

As a general rule, you should tip the dealer up to and no more than three times an hour, *and only if you are winning*. No dealer will expect you to tip if you are losing. So how much and how do you tip? If you are placing bets of ten dollars, it is a good idea to place a tip/bet for the dealer of one dollar. A good rule is to tip one-tenth of your bet two to three times an hour—but again, *only if you are winning!*

Now, you do not just hand the dealer the tip; *instead, you place a bet for him*. This is easy, and there is more than one reason for doing so. First, place your bet, and then directly in front of your bet place your tip. If you win, the dealer also wins and effectively doubles his tip.

This serves two purposes. First, it is the proper and nice thing to do.

And second, if you place a bet for the dealer, he then has a stake in your play and *wants you to win*. Do not underestimate this! Dealers rely on tips to supplement their incomes. If you are nice to the dealer, the dealer and the pit boss will be nice to you. I recall playing at the Sands Atlantic City in the upstairs high-limit pit a few years ago with a very nice female dealer. Well, she so appreciated my tips that several times during the session, when I had a toke out for her and actually lost, she would pay me (and of course herself) anyway, just so she got the tip! This has actually happened to me several times throughout the years. Pretty cool, huh?

Remember not to overtip!

This is a biggie! You never want to overtip, because it will cut into your edge. Stick to my advice on tipping.

This leads me to comps.

Comp stands for "complimentary"; it's a gift from the casino for your play. I urge you to take advantage of them. *Always have your play rated.* Usually when you sit down and buy in, the pit boss or the dealer will ask you if you have a comp card or if you want your play rated. Do it! You will get free rooms, free meals, free show tickets, and all kinds of other free things that can be rightly considered as part of your winnings. In Las Vegas, the casinos give away comps like nobody's business. In Atlantic City, it is not as easy to get them, especially weekend or holiday room comps, unless you are a high roller—or a big loser, which is usually the case. The island casinos—well, unless you are a true high roller or really big loser, don't expect *any* free rooms. Meals are a different story: usually two hours of play at ten dollars a hand is enough to get you lunch.

What about casino dress? Unfortunately, the reality is that there is no dress code in the casino. But I believe that if you look like a winner, you will think and act like a winner, and subsequently your chances of winning will go up. Yet you will see many very poorly dressed individuals in the casino. I recommend casual business attire, especially on the weekends or in the evening. Also, if you go to the casino for the purpose of making money playing blackjack, I suggest that you keep your mind on the game, keep socializing to a minimum, and try to get your mind off the opposite sex, or the same sex if you are so inclined for that matter. Whatever!

Remember, when you are in the casino, you are there for one reason: to make money! *Stay focused and avoid distractions.* If you are at the tables for a while and need a break, it is then that you can let your hair down for a while; but when break time is over, it is back to work.

Have you heard of *casino credit*? Yes, the nice casinos will extend to you a credit line! How good of them, isn't it? Be careful with this, however: it is all too easy to blow a bunch of hard cash real fast, especially if you are an unwise player with no discipline and do not play according to the strategy I am trying to teach you. Casino credit can actually be a good thing, if you are smart about it, because you will not have to bring a lot of cash with you to the casino; and the money they lend you is not charged a fee of any kind and has *no interest*. Now, the bad thing about casino credit is that the casino will be able to track your wins and losses very closely. If they see that you are winning more than you are losing, there is the chance that you can get yourself into trouble, especially in Las Vegas. Personally, I do not use casino credit, but if you are a high roller it may be smart. *Just be careful.*

A few more important words to the wise. Be an extra-smart player and do not advertise to people that you use the Gregorian Strategy, especially if confronted by a casino pit boss—again, especially in Las Vegas. There is always the chance that if you are in fact a proficient user of the Gregorian Strategy, you may get barred in Las Vegas or Reno. The chance is small, especially if you do not advertise it and play as I am telling you to, *but it is real*. If a pit boss asks you anything about your play, just say, "I play according to how I feel at the time. Sometimes I hit, and sometimes I stand."

Lastly, be aware of the fact that the casino is full of professional pickpockets and other riffraff who will go to great lengths to separate you from your money. When you take out your money for your buy-in, do it while holding your hands and money under the table, and do not buy in for a large sum. If you do win a lot of money at the table, again be careful, and ask the pit boss to give you a marker it. A marker is like a casino check made out in your name that you take to the casino cage; only you can cash it. Do this because, believe me, there will be people watching you leave the table with stacks of chips, and it will be all too easy for them to pick your pocket. Most casino pickpockets operate at night or on weekends when the casino is full.

I had a run-in with a pickpocket once. I was playing at Bally's Wild West casino in Atlantic City and it was late. I had just walked over from Caesars, down the boardwalk a bit. Well, I sat down to play at Bally's only for a short while and cashed in my chips—just a few hundred. Then I put the money with my other cash, which totaled four thousand dollars deep in my right front pocket. I began to walk through the casino on my way back to the Claridge, where I was staying that night. Well, I got back to my room, and as I got ready for bed, I reached into my pocket . . . and the money was gone! All of it! I had never felt a thing, nothing whatsoever. It was a real wake-up call for me. These people are good, very good. Also, if you drive up to the casino, have your car valet-parked. This way you will not have to walk any distance to your car. Be smart in and out of the casino.

♣ | *7* | ♦

A Blackjack Diary

Atlantic City

This is a real account of a week's play in Atlantic City, transcribed here as I wrote it down on a notepad in the casinos. It should serve as a real-time version of what you can expect from a week of play in an actual casino using the Gregorian Strategy.

Day one. Sunday. It is 5:00 PM. I just arrived here in Atlantic City after my hour's drive up. I am a little hungry right now, and I am actually writing this while I am in the casino of Caesars, sitting at the bar just inside the main entrance. I am planning to play blackjack for a few hours tonight, so I don't want to eat anything too heavy as it will make me tired. I am going to walk upstairs and get a slice of pizza. I am alone today. I must say that this casino is very beautiful; I really enjoy walking around inside it.

5:45 PM. All right now, pizza is down and I am ready to go out and scout the tables. The casino is reasonably crowded tonight; all the blackjack pits are open. You know, sometimes when the casino is not that full, they close one of the pits here. Many large casinos do the same thing. The casinos want their tables full. They will make more money per hour with full tables, which makes sense from a business point of view. Now I am going to casually walk around the blackjack tables and observe the games. The rules here are pretty standard as Atlantic City rules go. The game offered here is an eight-deck game, dealer stands on all 17s, double on any two cards allowed, double after split allowed, split up to four times, split aces draw only one card, and no surrender. Now, if you guys read my book and were paying attention, *tell me*, why am I not just sitting down at *any* table to play? Right, I am looking for a table with a positive bias—that is, a game in which I observe that the dealer is not winning every hand while the players are losing their shirts. I want to find a game where the players appear to be winning. So I will observe the game, preferably from the start of the deal just after a new shuffle through ten consecutive hands. If the dealer appears to be winning more than 50 percent of his hands, I will walk to another table and start over again. Also, I usually play at $25-minimum tables. I do this because I can. You play at whatever level is appropriate for you. You did read the money management section of this book, didn't you?

6:30 PM. I sat down to play in the back pit, end table. I sat at first base, which just happens to be my favorite seat. It really does not matter where you sit. I just feel comfortable there, I guess from my card-counting days. Twenty-five-dollar minimum. As luck would have it, I was dealt a blackjack the first hand; now, don't tell me that scouting tables for biases does not matter! I played through the first shoe with three other players. The guy at third base made a comment one time when I did not split my aces when the dealer had a 10 up. Well, I decided to hit them according to the Gregorian Strategy, and this *is* the correct play. I was dealt a 2. If I had split them, my first hand would now have been either 13 or 3, a *very* bad hand when playing against a 10, as we know. According to the rules here at Caesars, split aces draw only one card. Well, my total with my two aces and my 2 dealt was now 14, *a soft 14 obviously*, so I took another card—a 6! Excellent, I now had a total of 20; this gave me a very good chance of winning. If I had split the aces, according to old basic strategy, I would have been stuck with a soft 13 and a soft 17, two very lousy hands when playing against a dealer 10. Well, the dealer flipped over a 7 for a total of 17. *I won.* Again, if I had split my aces, in this case I would have lost one hand and pushed the other; net loss would have been $25. I guess I did the right thing. The guy in third shut up real fast. At the end of the first shoe, approximately twenty minutes, I was up $100—not much, really, only four bets as I am playing a $25 minimum. Here at Caesars Atlantic City, they use a shuffle machine with two distinct and separate decks of cards. So when the dealer began to deal this deck, I did not play the first few hands. You can usually get away with this for three or four hands; then you will either have to bet or leave the table. Again, I was observing the deck in an attempt to find a positive bias. As luck would have it, the dealer won the first three hands. Time to find another table. I took my hundred-dollar win and split. That is discipline, baby, in action!

7:00 PM. If you do what I just did—run off the table after observing it for a few hands and leaving—do yourself this favor: walk to another pit for a while and remember, you do not want to bring any unwanted attention to yourself. In fact, it is a nice night out tonight, so I will walk out the back of Caesars and take the boardwalk over to the Wild West casino.

It really is beautiful here tonight; it is clear, the casinos are all lit up so nicely, you can hear the sound of the surf, there are people all walking around. Ah yes, I do love this!

7:45 PM. I was ready for more action! I scouted the tables and sat down to play. Here at the Wild West, the rules are identical to those I found at Caesars: eight-deck game, dealer stands on all 17s, double on any two cards, double after split allowed, split up to four times, split aces draw only one card and no surrender. Well, as luck would have it, it was not me this time, but the dealer who got blackjack on the first hand I sat down to play; that is just the way it is. No big deal. I was playing with a full table this time, so the game was going more slowly after the first shoe; I was only up $50 for the night, having lost back $50 of the $100 I had won at Caesars. At this particular table, there was no shuffle machine, and with the full table, the game was not progressing fast enough for me. I figured I would play through another shoe and if the action did not improve, I would leave the table. The guy next to me was blowing smoke practically in my face, and I was finding this quite annoying. Keeping true to form, I sat out the first few hands, which sometimes upsets other players, *but I really could not care less and neither should you!* This shoe went very well. I had two opportunities to split and double down according to the Gregorian Strategy, which I won, and I also received a blackjack. During this shoe, I won back the $50 I had lost of the $100 I had won at Caesars, plus I won another $75, so my net to this point was $175. Not bad. I decided to play here a little longer. I ended up playing through six shoes total at that particular table, seven shoes altogether so far; approximate time invested at this point: three and a half hours. I picked up another $25 at that table.

It is now 8:30 and I am $200 ahead for the night so far—nothing spectacular at all, but it beats a sharp stick in the eye, as my dad says. I am hungry again—I had only one slice of pizza before—and so I just asked the pit boss for a comp for the buffet. I love buffets! Remember to always have your play rated! This is how you will get comps. You see, I can actually count this comp toward my winnings because I would have had to pay for it. He of course gave it to me because I play here a lot! Well, off to the buffet!

11:30 PM. After dinner, I was off going to hit the casino in Bally's. I was a little tired, so unless I found a hot table I was ready to call it a night soon. At around 10:00 PM, after checking out the tables looking for a positive bias, I sat down to play at a table in the middle blackjack pit. I just happened to know the dealer, whose name was Steve. I had played with him several times in the past. If I am familiar with a dealer, I will often ask how the cards are running. Dealers know if they are hot or cold. I strongly advise you to listen. If you ask a dealer if he is "hot" and he says yes, stay away from that table. If a dealer is "cold," that means there is a positive bias and you should sit down and play. This is another good reason to be good to the dealers and tip them when you are winning: their "inside information" is worth its weight in gold, *trust me*. To my delight, Steve told me that he was running cold, and that it might be a good time for me to play. *Remember*, the dealers really are on your side; they honestly want you to win in the hope that if you do, you will also take care of them in the form of a "toke" (tip), something I always do. So I sat down to play, sitting in the first-base position with three other players, $25 a hand. After the first shoe, I was running about even. Well, right at the beginning of the second shoe I began to have several consecutive wins. By midshoe, I was up another $350. At the end of the shoe, I lost $50 back. Honestly, I was tired, so I decided to quit for the night. It was around 11:00 PM, I was $500 to the good, and I was done. Steve was right! So keeping true to form, along with the several tokes I gave Steve through the game, I threw him another $10. His advice paid off. I really did not feel like driving an hour to get home, so I asked the pit boss to comp me a room for the night. I knew that I would have no problem getting a room comp—first of all it was a weeknight, and second of all I do play here all the time.

Right now I am in my comped room here at Bally's. The rooms here are nice and clean; I have a very nice view of the boardwalk from here as I look out the window. I have a nice king-sized bed, cable TV, a nice view, and it is all for free! Ah yes, life is good!

Let me summarize this first day of play. I have been here for about six hours, played for about four of them, and I am up $500 cash. I also got the buffet comped, a $15 value, and now a room, a $65 value. Total winnings, including comps for the day, are $580. Today was a very decent day so far because I played for only about four hours. With comps, I made $145 per hour of play, playing $25 a hand. Without counting my comps, I am at this point way over my theoretical win rate, and as such I know that

I will lose some back; that is just the way it is when you do this for a living.

I am going to watch some TV now, and try to get some sleep. I will write more when I get up. 'Bye.

Day two. Monday. It is 4:30 AM. I never get up this early, I truly hate getting up early, but I am getting pretty excited writing about a week of my playing in Atlantic City. Honestly, I wish I were in Las Vegas right now, but you can't have it all.

5:45 AM. I am showered, dressed, and ready to go, the sun is just coming up, and, as I look out the window, the reflection on the ocean is just beautiful. Atlantic City is really a beautiful place.

I need coffee! I will walk through this casino over to the Wild West casino; there is a little coffee shop there in the casino.

6:30 AM. I turned in my key at the front desk, checked out, and now am sitting at the coffee shop at the Wild West. As I sit here with my coffee, I am looking around at this place; it really is nice in here. The casino is relatively empty right now; this is good because perhaps I will be able to find a game with few—or even better—*no* other players. Playing one-on-one with the dealer allows you to get in more hands per hour; and theoretically, because of your advantage using the Gregorian Strategy, your win rate per hour should go up. I will take my coffee and walk around the blackjack pits.

Just looking over from here, I can see several completely empty tables. I am going over to play for a while. The only problem with walking up to an empty table is you will not be able to look for biases. You will hear me talk about biases a lot, but because I will be playing alone, hopefully my theoretical advantage will make up the difference. Let's see what happens.

9:00 AM. At 7:00 AM I sat down to play at an empty table; now I am now back at the coffee shop so I can write this. For the entire two hours of play, I was able to play alone. When I sat down to play, the table was a $5 minimum, and as I said there were several empty tables. In the morning, especially with few players in the casino, most if not all of the tables will have low minimum bets. As the day goes on and the casino gets more crowded, you will notice the table minimums going up. As you know, I play $25 a hand most of the time, never less, sometimes more. I feel comfortable at this rate of play. So what I did was, since I was the only player at the table and I play there all the time, I asked the pit boss to raise the table minimum to $25. This would keep most people away from the table; most people would rather play at the lower-minimum tables. The pit boss took my comp card as I bought in; *my buy-in for the game was $400*. He checked my card and, as he returned, took off the red $5 minimum card and replaced it with a green $25. Now I was happy! He wished me luck and returned my comp card. The dealer changed my cash for chips and I was ready. Playing alone has so many advantages: more hands per hour, fewer distractions, and fewer bigmouth players who make really dumb comments about your strategy. Remember, most players, *at least at this point*, are still using the old basic strategy and will not understand your plays since you will be using the Gregorian Strategy. Let them say what they want and watch who leaves the table with more chips. *Believe me*, it will be you a majority of the time.

In my two hours of play one-on-one with the dealer, I was averaging about one hundred hands per hour, so in theory, I should have been winning one percent of all the money I put into play. Again theoretically, playing $25 a hand times one hundred hands, that should come out to around $25 per-hour win rate. Well, after the two hours and after toking the dealer, I walked off the table $337.50 to the good. That was still way above my expected win rate; but you must remember, we are talking about the long run here. What that means is, I knew I could not go on winning at this high rate, sooner or later I would lose. It was a mathematical certainty. Since last night, I am up $837.50 cash, and $80 in comps. Actually, before I left the last table, I asked the pit boss for a comp for the breakfast buffet, so that is another $8.

Thus, $837.50 + $80 + $8 = $925.50. Not bad for six hours of "work." Off to the buffet!

11:00 AM. I am at the Sands casino right now. I am in point of fact sitting in front of a slot machine. God forbid that I would ever put a nickel in one these things. They are for the birds, and I want you to forget about them altogether. I am just using it to rest my notepad on. That is all these things are good for, if you ask me.

The casino is usually crowded down here, and I rarely play in the blackjack pits because of that. Upstairs is nicer to play and usually not as crowded. All right, upstairs we will go. I will scope out the games first, as usual. In the upstairs pit at the time of this writing, you will find a four-deck game with standard Atlantic City rules: that is, dealer stands on all 17s, double on any two cards, double after split allowed, split up to four times, split aces draw only one card, and no surrender. I sit down to play with a dealer I know well, named Bee; I often call her "Killer" Bee. Bee is one of the nicest dealers I happen to know, but for some reason she is just tough to beat. Bee's table has a $15 minimum and I again find first base open. I buy in for $400. Bee's table is often full because people like her. I play at Bee's table for an hour and in that hour I lose $200! I told you, *I don't call her Killer Bee for nothing.* I tell Bee that I am leaving because she is killing me, but it really has nothing to do with her personally. So, seven hours of play and I am still ahead $637.50 cash.

12:30 PM. This place is getting crowded. *This is another reason why I like Las Vegas better*—Vegas never gets as crowded as Atlantic City. I am off to the Claridge.

The Claridge offers the best game in Atlantic City. At the Claridge, you will find all the standard Atlantic City rules along with surrender and, if you play upstairs at the high-limit pit, they also offer resplit aces. That is where I am going, to the high-limit pit.

1:45 PM. I am again sitting at one of these one-armed bandits and using it to write on. Really, stay away from these things— trust me on this. In a minute, I am going to walk upstairs to the high-limit area. The games in this area are four-deck games, and the rules are as follows: dealer stands on all 17s, double on any two cards, double after spit allowed, split up to four times, *including* aces, and surrender is offered. These are very similar to the common rules that you will find in Las Vegas, and theoretically, your advantage using the Gregorian Strategy will go up. In Las Vegas, the dealer usually hits soft 17. In the high-limit area at the Claridge, you will find games with $100 and $50 minimums. I will play at a $50 minimum table. When playing at this rate, you have to be very careful. Playing $50 a hand can hurt you pretty fast if you are not careful and have no discipline, but you know about that already so I do not have to worry about you, right? I will definitely observe these games before I sit down to play. In the high-limit pit, as I said before, the games are all four-deck and there are no shuffle machines. What I will do, and I strongly recommend that you do the same, is watch the table through ten hands to see which way the bias seems to be going. Here I go. I will write more in a while.

6:00 PM. I just finished a rather lengthy session playing about three and a half hours straight and finishing up only $50. At one point I was down $300 of my winnings, but I fought my way back and then some. I am getting hungry now, but what do I want to eat? I know, I will walk back over to the Sands casino. There is a place in there called the Bo-Koo lounge; excellent food! I am of course going to ask for a comp, so I will walk over to a pit boss, give him my comp card, and ask him if I "rate" one—*I obviously know that I do*. I in fact play here a few times a week, and at $25 a hand, you can usually get what you want if you play enough, which I definitely do. Plus, I am friendly with the pit bosses and most of them kind of know me. I will try to find someone I am familiar with. I will write more when I get to the restaurant.

7:00 PM. I got the comp to the Bo-Koo lounge, like I thought I would, and I am ready to order. I will have the filet mignon. *Of course I will order the most expensive thing on the menu; wouldn't you? You should!* I will also have, for an appetizer, the shrimp cocktail please, and a glass of red house wine, thanks.

Let's recap this blackjack excursion: ten and a half hours of play, day two, and I am still up $687.50 cash, plus the comps—including this meal, which will come to about $35. That comes to $123 in comps, so my total is now $810.50. My food just arrived; I will write more later.

8:15 PM. What to do, what to do? Well, I think that I will go back to Caesars and see what is going on over there. I will write more when I get into the casino. It is a little rainy tonight so I will cut through the casino of the Sands, head over the little cross bridge that leads to the Claridge, walk quickly across the street and cut through the casino at Bally's that leads to the casino at the Wild West, then take the escalator over to the casino at Caesars. I will write when I get there.

8:45 PM. On my way walking over to Caesars, cutting through Bally's, I decided to stop and get a shoeshine. I find it very relaxing sitting and getting my shoes shined. You know, maybe I will just stay over here in Atlantic City again tonight; only problem is, I will need a change of clothes. No problem, I can hit some of the shops over at Caesars and pick up some stuff to wear. Before I shop I will ask for a room, comp obviously; why pay for something when you can just ask someone to just give it to you? Right? I will write some more later, when I get into my room.

10:55 PM. I just got settled into my room. I picked up some new clothes and a few other things I needed. This time I had gone to the front desk and asked for a comp room. Then the girl there ran my comp card, as they always do, and gave me this room. This room is nicer than the one at Bally's, except the view is lousy. No big deal, though, I have seen this place a thousand times anyway. Well, I am a bit tired right now and I am definitely done for the day. I am just going to watch some TV and go to sleep. I will write more when I get up in the morning. Good night.

Day three. Tuesday. Wow, it is 9:30 AM; I usually do not sleep this late. I was up watching TV kind of late, though, although I really cannot remember what the hell I was watching. I am hungry as usual, so I am going to get myself cleaned-up and ready to go. I will write more at breakfast.

10:30 AM. I am now at the breakfast buffet at Caesars. Honestly, this buffet is lousy—and I would not be upset about it, but I bought this one on my own. I was too lazy to ask for a comp. I really wish I had, though. I have been to this buffet many times before, and I really have to tell you straight, it could use some help . . . a lot of help, actually. The eggs are cold, the bacon tastes like rubber, and would you believe there is no toast! The coffee is all right, though. It is my fault because I know better, I should have gone over to the breakfast place at the Claridge. It is not a buffet but the food is very good. In an attempt to get even with this place for this truly lousy food, I am going to play here later on to see if I can take some of their money at the blackjack tables. I am going to finish my lousy food now so I will write more in a little bit.

11:15 AM. I am sitting in the casino now at a slot machine as I write this. The casino is reasonably quiet, and I should be able to find an empty or nearly empty table. *Remember*, empty or nearly empty tables are better because you will receive more hands per hour, and theoretically your chances of winning will go up. The more hands you play, the greater your chances of winning are when you use the Gregorian Strategy for multiple deck blackjack, unlike this slot machine—the more you play it, the greater are your chances of losing.

I am going to walk around the blackjack pits looking for a game now, so I will write more later.

1:30 PM. Well, things did not go as I had planned. Not only did I have to eat lousy food for breakfast from this place, but after playing for about an hour, I lost $125. I was playing at a table with two other players. I was sitting at third base, and although I did receive several blackjacks, I lost just about every double down I made and *that cost me*. It happens. Well, the day is still young and I am going to walk over to Trump casino now.

2:15 PM. I am now sitting on a bench on the boardwalk as I write. The sun is shining, although it is a little chilly out, but the air smells fresh, like the ocean. I just wanted to get a little clean air to help me wake up. Off to Trump!

3:00 PM. I am in the casino right now, sitting at one of these slot machines writing again. This place is a little crowded. I am hoping to win some money here today, so let's get to work. I am off to scout the tables.

6:00 PM. The blackjack game offered here at Trump is a six-deck game in which the dealer stands on all 17s; you can double on any two cards. Double after split allowed, split aces draw only one card, any other card may be split up to four times, and no surrender—basically standard Atlantic City rules. After playing for almost three hours at one table, Lady Luck smiled on me and I walked away from the table with $350. I was playing first base with one other person for the first hour, $25 minimum as usual, and the game was going nice and fast. Then two other players joined me at the table and the game slowed down. Actually, when I first sat down to play I quickly lost another $75 and was starting to feel a little depressed, but halfway through the second shoe I began to make a strong comeback. Just before the other two players arrived, I had gotten about $200 ahead, and just before I decided to quit, two more players were about to sit down. I was already up the $350 and I thought that they would really slow the game down so I decided to leave, also *as usual*. I am hungry again and I know just where I am going to eat. I am going to go out to the boardwalk and take a buggy ride down to Hooters! For those of you who do not know Atlantic City, you will find these neat buggy rides on the boardwalk itself. Generally the buggies and their operators are very nice men, sometimes women; for a few bucks you can get a ride down the boardwalk if you do not feel like walking. You will find many of these buggies out on the boardwalk on any given day or night. Many times they hang out just outside the casinos. Today is a little chilly out, and from Trump casino, realistically, it is a long walk (*for me*) to the Tropicana in which Hooters is found. Come on, you have to admit they do have the *bust*—I mean best!—hot wings on the planet. *With regard to that last sentence, I really did write "bust" first. It must be one of those Freudian slips. Can you do that while you are writing? I guess so, right?*

6:45 PM. It is dark out and I am in a little buggy on my way to the Trop and Hooters to eat. Let's recap the financial situation so far. This is day three, approximately fourteen and a half hours of play. I was ahead $687.50 cash from yesterday; then I lost $125 at Caesars this morning; then I won $350 at Trump. That puts me at plus $912.50 cash. I also received the comped room last night at Caesars, a $70 value, so let's add all the comps. Before last night's room, I was given $123 in comps, now adding the $70 room from Caesars, that makes $193 in comps. My total is $1,105.50, which includes both cash and comps. Not bad at all for fourteen and a half hours of "work." It is hard to write in this buggy, so I will write more in a little while, 'bye.

7:30 PM. I am sitting at the table in Hooters and I just ordered ten hot wings, breaded with Three Mile Island sauce with blue cheese dressing on the side, curly fries, and a Coke. I *never* drink when I am either planning to or actually playing blackjack, and neither should you! If you get buzzed or drunk, you will undoubtedly make mistakes when you play. It will cost you, so don't do it. When the cute little waitress comes over to ask you if you want a drink at the tables, which will be about every twenty minutes, give or take, get a cup of coffee instead, or a soda. Work now and play later. After I finish eating, I am going to hit the casino here at the Tropicana for a while. You know, I think I am going to stay over in Atlantic City again! Why not? I miss my dog, though; my girlfriend is taking care of him right now. He is a little Boston terrier named Buster and he is just the cutest thing. Food is here, got to go.

8:30 PM. I am done eating and off to hit the blackjack tables for a while. Here at the Tropicana, you will find eight-deck games in which the dealer will stand on all 17s, double on any two cards is allowed, double after splitting is allowed, split aces draw only one card, no resplit aces, split any other card up to four times. As I said before, here in Atlantic City, all of the casinos here have adopted the same rules except for the Clairdge, which also offers surrender and resplit aces in their high-limit games. This makes the Claridge the best place to play blackjack in Atlantic City. As I have said several times in this book, you will always want to find blackjack games in casinos offering the most liberal rules. Now the problem is, *with me especially*, since I play blackjack as a full-time job at this point, I cannot overstay my welcome at any one casino. *This is why*, as you can see by reading this account of my blackjack forays, I jump from casino to casino. Also remember that if you play in Las Vegas, your potential for making money using the Gregorian Strategy will go up because, in general, the rules offered for the blackjack games are better, being very similar to those offered by the Claridge's high-limit games.

9:00 PM. I am sitting in the lounge just up the escalators from Hooters. The casino is busy right now, which is not good from a moneymaking standpoint. If the tables are full, the game will progress more slowly, so it will take longer to make the same money. I am going to check out the tables now, again looking for a table with a positive bias and as few players as possible. I will write more later.

11:30 PM. I am back at the lounge again, this time having a margarita on the rocks with salt—my favorite drink. I found a table with just one other player whom I am sure was a card counter; he was sitting at third base. It is easy for an ex–card counter like myself to spot another one within a few minutes of his starting play. As a general rule, card counters will sit either at first or third base. The reason is that as the cards are dealt out, you do not have to move your head to see all the cards, and if you are really good, you will not move your eyes much either. This guy was not so good; he made it pretty obvious that he was looking at all the cards dealt; I wish him luck whoever he was. I just want to say something here—no need to put your thinking caps on or anything—but in my experience I have known of only two women who were card counters, and only one of them was actually any good at it. Why, I do not know. Many women do play this game. I have always said that if a woman were to learn this game at the level of a professional, she would make a million dollars. The reason is that the casinos, I believe, are less apt to consider a woman to actually be a professional blackjack player, and thus would be less apt to bother her.

All right, back to business. I played for about two hours at that table and picked up another $75. During my play, there were several instances where I was dealt a hard 12 against dealer up cards of 4, 5, and 6, and when I asked the dealer for a hit, he tried to correct me, saying that the book says to stand. I was thinking, *That's what you think*; he was obviously referring to a book on the old basic strategy. Now, as we know, according to the Gregorian Strategy we are supposed to hit these hard 12s, right? You were paying attention earlier in the book, weren't you? Anyway, each time I hit my hard 12, I was "lucky" enough to catch a card that put me right in the 17–21 range, in fact, I once caught a 9 on a hard 12, which gave me 21! I think the dealer was impressed. Sometimes you will not be so lucky, for there will be times when you bust your stiff hands when the old strategy says stand. Believe me, *trust the Gregorian Strategy*, over the long run you will win making these types of plays. Are you still with me?

12:30 AM. I am ready to hit the tables once again. I am not tired and I am not drunk or buzzing; I only had the one drink. You know, looking around this place really makes me realize how much I love the casino atmosphere and this particular lifestyle. All right, off to the tables. I wish myself luck.

2:30 AM. I am again back at the lounge. I went back to that same table. Our friend the card counter was not there this time. I was playing with two other folks, $25 minimum. I sat at the first seat next to first base and picked up another $150. I also got a comped room. I am tired now and I have a bit of a headache. I am going to go up to the room now; I will write more then.

3:15 AM. I am in my room now. Let's recap so far. Cash, I am up $1,137.50 including tonight's winnings. I also got another room comp, which is $60 at the Trop. That makes $253 in comps. Total hours of play in these three days are eighteen and a half. That puts my hourly cash rate at about $61.50 per hour, playing at $25 a hand. At this point I am still over my projected win rate, but if you notice, at one point I was making $145 per hour—that was at the end of day one. My win rate playing $25 a hand using the Gregorian Strategy perfectly should be around $25 per hour, which is estimating one hundred hands per hour winning 1 percent of that money wagered under standard Atlantic City rules. If I am receiving more than an average of one hundred hands per hour, I will win more; if I am receiving less than one hundred hands per hour, I will win less, *on average.* So my win rate of $145 had to go down, and so will my current rate of $61.50. It is an unavoidable mathematical fact. That said I am going to sleep.

Day four. Wednesday. It is now 10:30 AM. I am all cleaned-up and ready to go. I am going to hit the buffet for breakfast after I check out.

11:45 AM. I am at the buffet. I paid for this one; I should have asked for a comp for it last night, but I forgot. The food here is better than at Caesars—actually almost anything is better than that buffet. What is the plan for the day? I think I will hit the casino here at the Tropicana for a while and take it from there.

12:30 PM. I am in the casino now, it is not as busy as last night and I can see from the slot machine where I am writing, that there are several empty tables. All right, here I go. Although I am going to play at one of the empty tables, and doing so will deny me the luxury of gaining any knowledge of biases, I am hoping that some one-on-one play, which will give me more hands per hour, will make up for it.

2:30 PM. Down $100. I found a $25-minimum table and got some one-on-one play but lost $100 in about two hours. I am going to go back to the Claridge and see if I can turn this around.

I haven't been outside yet but it looks very nice. It is a long walk back to the Claridge, but the fresh air may do me good.

3:15 PM. It is nice out! Very nice out, actually. I am sitting on a bench outside the Wild West casino right now. There are lots of people out enjoying the day—don't any of them work? I know they all couldn't play blackjack for a living like me! Well, I am going to just sit here for a minute just to take this all in. I really like to watch people. People are very interesting, don't you think? I look at them and wonder who they are and what they do. Enough of that. Let's hit the Claridge and play some blackjack!

4:00 PM. I am in the lobby of the Claridge at the phone; I just had to call home to check up on things. I do not (and I refuse to) carry a cell phone, but maybe I should get one. I am going into the casino now; I am not going to play the high-limit game like last time. I am going to hit the standard game, $25 minimum. The casino is busy now, bummer. I will write more later.

6:00 PM. Not a good day so far—I lost another $175. That makes today's losses $275 so far. I hope this streak ends soon. I am hungry again; I am going over to the Sands now via the walkway that connects the two casinos. I will stop at the Chinese food place on the way; lousy food, but it is convenient.

6:30 PM. I am at the Chinese place. I am not surprised about my losses today; like I said, it was inevitable, as I was over my win rate. I am going to finish up this soup and hit the Sands casino.

7:15 PM. I am at the Sands in the upstairs blackjack pit. I saw my friend Bee dealing blackjack up here, but I am not going to play with her today. I love her as a person, but she is always tough for me to beat. I wonder, could she possibly be a card shark? No way, right? Hey, you never know. Right now I am sitting at this Yahtzee slot machine—you played the game as a kid, didn't you? This game looks cute but as you know I would never play it. Slot machines of any kind are a no-no. I am off to the blackjack tables.

10:30 PM. After scouting out the tables looking for biases, I ended up finding a table at the downstairs pit, believe it or not. It seemed like all the tables in the upstairs pit had negative biases, and as such I wanted to avoid them. After playing in the back downstairs pit for about two and a half hours at $25 a hand, I had won $150. Hopefully that losing trend is over now. I am not done yet, though; I want to play awhile more. I am going to go back to the tables for a while.

12:30 PM. I am sitting at the Yahtzee game again writing this. I just finished playing with a dealer I know named Lyle, a very nice guy. After playing for about an hour and a half, I finished up a measly $37.50. But a win is better than a loss anytime, so I will take it and not complain. I also got a comp for a room here, a $65 value. I am tired and I am going up to the room.

1:15 AM. End of day four. Well, today was not a good day, but it must be expected and believe me, losses, *sometimes consecutive ones*, will happen. Let's recap. Twenty-six hours of play so far. I am up $1,050 cash, and including this room, my total comp value is $318. My hourly cash win rate is now approximately $40.50. Still over my projected win rate at $25 a hand. Actually, I did play for a few hours at $50 a hand at the Claridge on day one or two, so that may contribute to my higher average.

Time to watch some TV and catch some shut-eye. Good night.

Day five. Thursday. They gave me a room with a hot tub here at the Sands and I took full advantage of it this morning. So, here I am in the hot tub watching TV, livin' large! I even ordered room service and told them to charge it to the room, I have never done this before and I will see what happens when I check out (remember, this room was comped). I wonder if they will comp the room service? We shall see. Well, I am dressed and ready for more casino blackjack action! It is 11:00 AM and I am going to hit the casino here at the Sands for a while and see what happens. I will write more from the casino after I check out.

Noon. I checked out with no problems; they took care of the room service, also comped! Not bad . . . that was a $40 breakfast! I ordered everything, plus it was brought to me in my room! I am going to have to do this more often. I am sitting in the casino right now at a slot machine in the downstairs casino. I am going to play here for a while so I am off to check out the games. I will write more when I get back.

4:45 PM. Remember what I said about not leaving a winning table? Well, I listened to my own advice for a change and in four hours of play at $25 a hand I won $337.50. Not so bad. I was playing at first base with two and sometimes three other players and two different dealers. I only left the game because they changed the cards; otherwise I would have just kept on playing. I once stayed at a table for fourteen hours straight—actually, that was right here at the Sands a few years ago, during my card-counting days. I had my little cutie with me and she was about to freak out on me so I had to leave. I am going to walk down the boardwalk a bit to Resorts casino. I will write more when I get there.

5:00 PM. I am at Resorts. This place was actually the first casino to open in Atlantic City; the Claridge came soon after. The Resorts casino is also the same casino that the late Ken Uston took to court after being barred for counting cards a few years ago. This resulted in a landmark decision preventing all of the New Jersey casinos of Atlantic City from barring anyone from playing blackjack for possessing advanced skill at the game. Thanks, Ken. R.I.P.

The Resorts hotel-casino and the Claridge hotel-casino still possess that Old World charm lacking in most of the modern casinos down here, or is it up here? Where am I, anyway?

5:30 PM. I am going to hit the tables—*play*, that is, I never *actually* hit the tables, although I have seen many people do so over the years after they lost all their money. Don't these people realize that inanimate objects have no feelings? And more than likely, they only hurt themselves by doing it.

Here at Resorts casino, you will find an eight-deck game with standard Atlantic City rules, no surrender and no resplit Aces. I am going to go and observe the games for a while before I sit down to play.

7:00 PM. After just over an hour of play, I am down $125. I was playing at third base, $25 minimum, with two other players. I am going to take a little break and grab a hot dog or something, and then I am going to try this place again.

8:00 PM. Instead of getting a hot dog, I decided to get coffee and a doughnut. I am sitting at a little café in the casino as I write this. When I finish this food, I am going back to the tables once again. I have been running into long runs of bad hands. This will happen from time to time, trust me. All you can do is ride it out and keep on playing.

10:00 PM. I just finished playing for another hour and a half here at Resorts. I lost again—down another $175 playing $25 a hand. That makes today's losses here at Resorts $300. I did get a room comp here tonight. I think I am going to quit for the night, watch TV and make a few phone calls. I will write more from my room.

11:00 PM. Thursday. I am in my room now at Resorts. Let's recap this five-day excursion so far. Today I got my butt kicked at Resorts. That's life in the world of a professional blackjack player like myself. Cash earned so far? I was up $1,050 cash from yesterday, and I picked up another $337.50 at the Sands earlier today, which brings me to $1,387.50. Then I lost $300 here at Resorts, which brings me down to $1,087.50 cash won so far in thirty-two and a half hours, approximately. That is an hourly win rate of $33.50. Now, that is about where I am theoretically supposed to be, figuring on one hundred hands per hour, give or take. My comped total for this whole session so far is $318 plus the $40 room service at the Sands, plus this room here at Resorts, $60. That comes to $418 total in comps. Do you see why I always have my play rated? You had better do the same.

Day six. Friday. I am up and ready to go; it is 10:00 AM. I am going to hit the coffee shop then head over to the Trump Taj. I will write more from the coffee shop.

10:45 AM. I just checked out, and here I sit in the coffee shop eating a doughnut and drinking a cup of coffee. I have been here in Atlantic City for five days; I am starting my sixth today. From here the Taj is just a short walk away. I can use the fresh air. I am going to finish this coffee and I will be on my way.

11:15 AM. I am out on the boardwalk now sitting on a bench. It is a little cloudy, but the temperature is around fifty. I am wearing a light jacket so I am comfortable. The sea air smells so good. I am hoping to have a good day today, so let's go and see what happens.

Noon. I am inside the casino at the Taj. This place is really like a Las Vegas Strip resort. It is full of places to eat and shop and the casino is huge. The blackjack game offered here is an eight-deck, with standard Atlantic City rules, no surrender and no resplit Aces. The casino is reasonably busy now. I am going to scope out the tables. I will write more later.

2:00 PM. Now I am happy! I just finished playing on a $25-minimum table, playing first base with one other player, and I picked up $375 in just about an hour and a half. Although I did not get too many really good hands, the dealer kept on busting. The other guy sitting at the table was using old basic strategy, but he also did well. I only left the table because they changed the cards—bummer. I am going back to the tables for a while.

5:30 PM. I am hungry again. I just finished playing for about three hours with two other players, me playing third base. After some wild swings in my bankroll—at one point during the game I was down $200, and another time I was up $175—I finished only $25 ahead. In this case, because the game was really running with wild up-and-down swings, I should have quit when I was up the $175. But on a good note, I got a comp to the Safari Steak House restaurant—excellent atmosphere, great service, and the food is tops. I am going up there now. I will write more from the restaurant.

6:15 PM. I am sitting at my table in the back. This place is packed, and it is Friday night. Decisions, decisions, what will I eat? I must say, the grilled swordfish sounds very good, but I love a steak. I will flip a coin, heads = swordfish and tails = steak. It is heads, so swordfish it is! Appetizer? Shrimp cocktail. Can I also have a glass of your house wine, *red please?*

7:30 PM. Dinner is done. It was truly delicious. Now I am going to go back to The Claridge to play at their high-limit game for a little while. I really don't feel like walking at night on the boardwalk from the Taj; it is a long walk. I will go out to the boardwalk and take a buggy ride.

8:00 PM. I am in the buggy now. It is a little cold out but the buggy is enclosed, so it is not that bad. I am on my way to the Claridge's high-limit tables. *Remember*, these tables not only offer surrender, but also offer resplit Aces—definitely the best game in Atlantic City. Another reason I am going to play at the high-limit tables for a while is that I want them to give me a room comp. This is sometimes not so easy here in Atlantic City on the weekend. The Claridge is a smaller casino, plus I play there all the time, sometimes high limit, sometimes not. I am pretty sure that they will give it to me.

8:30 PM. I am at the Claridge in the casino sitting at a slot machine next to the stairs leading to the high-limit pit. I am going up there now. I will write more later.

Midnight. Almost three hours of play at $50 a hand with two other players, me at first base. I won $50, *one bet.* But I did get the room! I am in it now. When I checked in I asked if there were any rooms with a Jacuzzi, and the nice girl said, "Let me see, sir . . . Yes!" This room is huge, nice view of the boardwalk and ocean. Before I get in the Jacuzzi, let's recap up to this point. My hours of play are thirty-nine. I am plus $1,537.50 cash, and comps to date $531. My cash win rate is now approximately $39.50 per hour. This is about right, because I did put in several hours of play today and a couple of days ago at the high-limit, $50-minimum tables.

I am going to hit the Jacuzzi, watch some TV, and go to sleep. *Life is good.*

Day seven. Saturday, 10:30 AM. I am dressed and ready to hit the tables. Today is my last day of this little blackjack excursion. So far I have really enjoyed writing everything down for you. I hope you have also. I am going to hit the casino at the Sands this morning after I get some food at the Sands buffet next door. I am going to check out of the hotel here now, and I will write more from the buffet.

11:30 AM. This buffet is very interesting. It is called the Epic buffet. In here you will not only find reasonably good food, but also find the place covered from ceiling to floor with real movie props used in the movies *The Ten Commandments* and *Cleopatra*. It is very cool. I am going to finish my food then hit the casino.

12:15 PM. I am in the casino, second floor here at the Sands. The casino is getting pretty full already. I am going to check out the tables now and play for a while.

2:00 PM. I just lost $75 in about an hour and a half, playing $25 minimum. I just could not make a hand, which happens sometimes. I am going back for a while.

3:30 PM. Luck is not on my side so far; I am down another $50 in another hour or so of play. I am going to try Caesars casino. It is nice out, so I will hit the boardwalk and stroll over.

4:15 PM. I am at the casino in Caesars. It is very crowded, which is the main reason I do not like to play weekends here in Atlantic City. This will be my last hurrah, as I have to drive home today. Let's see if we can end this thing on an upward note.

7:00 PM. All right, I picked up another $175 in three hours of play, and I am happy. I am also tired and of course *hungry*. I am actually getting a little tired of this place; I never play this many days in a row. I am going to cash in these chips, get my car, and get outta here. Let me recap this whole thing now that I am certainly done. Total hours played: forty-five. Total cash won: $1,587.50. Total comps: $531. My hourly cash win rate was $35.25. If I add my comps to my total win, which I should rightly do because if I did not get those comps I would have had to pay for them, my total wins would be $2,118.50. That would bring my hourly total win rate to $47.

Time to get the car and go home, don't you think? I will hit a McDonald's on the way home. It is 7:30 PM. I should make it home by 9:00. That concludes this week in Atlantic City.

I really enjoyed detailing my week in Atlantic City . . . so much so that I decided to fly out to Las Vegas and do the same thing over there. Tomorrow I am flying out.

Las Vegas

Day one. I am leaving this morning for beautiful Las Vegas with my girlfriend. Today is Monday. We will be flying back Thursday night on the red-eye. If you go online, you can find some great package deals with hotels and various flights at really great prices at the last minute, like I did. It is 6:00 AM now, and we are off to the airport. We are leaving from Newark International Airport in New Jersey and we will arrive in the Vegas McCarran Airport at 10:30 AM Las Vegas time. We really have to get going.

10:35 AM Las Vegas time. We just touched down at McCarran Airport. I cannot believe that I actually slept just about the whole way. In fact, I only woke up once and I noticed that my girlfriend, sitting right next to me, was also sleeping with drool coming from the side of her mouth! She is going to hate me for writing that but so what, right? God only knows what I was doing during my sleep! I don't even want to think about it. I can see the Strip casinos from the airplane as we taxi to the terminal. Every time I come back to this place is like the first time—I truly, *truly* love it! Now for the rush out of the plane. *I hate this part*, everyone rushing to stand up and get his baggage and go nowhere fast. I just sit and calmly wait for most of the people to leave. I will just continue to sit here and write this. We are going to rent a car so we can get around easier. We know this place like the back of our hand—we used to live here, remember? I told you that. You forget everything, don't you . . .

Noon. We are now driving in the car we rented, a neat little Mustang convertible; yeah, we are cool! We are cruising with the top down, is there any other way to cruise with a convertible? The weather is perfect. When we left New York, it was about forty degrees; it is seventy degrees here in gorgeous Las Vegas today. We are on our way to the Golden Nugget downtown. I am just sitting here in the passenger's seat taking this all in while she does all the work driving. We could have taken the highway, but we decided to drive down Las Vegas Boulevard to take in the whole Las Vegas experience. We just passed the MGM Grand and the Luxor. The Excalibur is on our left, and behind us are Mandalay Bay and New York, New York. The traffic is light right now, but you can believe that tonight will be different. We are just passing the beautiful Bellagio now on our left; the Aladdin is on our right, and so is Paris Las Vegas. We are now passing the Flamingo and Caesars. The Barbary Coast is on our right. I can see Treasure Island from here, and also the Mirage. On our right, we are coming up on the Venetian; what an awesome place. The Stratosphere tower is clearly visible from here. We are passing the Stardust and the Riviera, coming up soon will be the Sahara. We are just going to keep cruising down Las Vegas Boulevard all the way downtown to the Golden Nugget, past the little wedding chapels.

All right, we just pulled up in front of the Golden Nugget; we brought one carry-on each. We are going to check in now so I will write more from our room.

1:45 PM. We are in our room, and now we both are hungry, *not just me this time*. We are going to take a walk down Fremont Street to the Golden Gate, where they have the most mouthwatering sixteen-ounce Porterhouse steak with all the trimmings for $7.77. It is the deal of the century.

2:30 PM. We are at the Golden Gate casino. If and when you come to Las Vegas, you have to visit this place. It is at the corner of Main Street and Fremont. This place really has stood still in time; it is a small casino full of that bygone-era charm. We are going to order our food now so I will write more later. Please, if you get a chance to go to the Golden Gate, say hello to Victor the waiter. You will recognize him because he kind of looks like Elvis. Hi Victor!

3:30 PM. We finished our steaks since, of course, we both just had to have one. I had mine medium-rare, of course, and it was perfect. Now I think we are going to go over to the Las Vegas Club right across the street to play some blackjack. Remember earlier when I was telling you about this place? Well, the Las Vegas Club has the best blackjack games probably *in the world* as of this writing. Their six-deck games offer surrender; you can resplit Aces or any other card as many times as you want; and you can double down on any number of cards.

4:00 PM. Here is the current plan: I am going to have my girlfriend scope out the tables with me; she knows how to find a positively biased table. You do remember about biases, don't you? She will work one side of the blackjack pit, and I will work the other. The casino here at the Las Vegas Club is small, so we can clearly see each other from across the pit. Hey, if you come here to the Las Vegas Club, check out the back of the casino, where you will find some very cool sports paraphernalia.

4:30 PM. She found a table. Now, she does not play, but she will run interference for the pit bosses if they try to give me a hard time (you remember when our discussion about heat, don't you?). It does not happen to me much now that I don't count cards anymore, but here in Las Vegas you have to be careful.

6:30 PM. In two hours of play at $25 a hand at the Las Vegas Club, I won $87.50. That paid for dinner and then some. I am happy. It is dark outside now and we are going to head over to the coffee shop at the Golden Nugget. Soon they will start the magnificent light show over Fremont Street. We will sit, have some coffee, and watch the show.

7:15 PM. We are at Starbucks at the Golden Nugget. I am drinking café mocha and my girlfriend is having a cappuccino.

The weather is just about perfect, and since it is Monday night, it is not that crowded. On the weekend there are a lot of people walking around. We are going to sit here at the coffee shop until after 8:00 PM so we can see the show, which is an animated light show with music. There are 1.2 million lights up there; very cool. It lasts for around ten or fifteen minutes, running every half hour or so to end around 10:30 PM. After this, we are going to the Golden Nugget for a while. I love the casino at the Golden Nugget; it is modern, but not too modern, and it still has some old Las Vegas charm left over. If you ever find yourself in the Golden Nugget, you have to check out the "Hand of Faith" exhibit near the lobby. The "Hand of Faith" is the largest natural piece of gold found to date. You will find it in a display case along with several other large pieces of gold. *Don't get any funny ideas, though.* I know you; I know what you are thinking about. Well, forget it! The exhibit is under constant surveillance, and I doubt that you would make it more than ten feet without getting caught. Also, just around the corner from the exhibit, you will find the high-limit blackjack pit. *Avoid playing in that pit.* I know that you are not counting cards using the Gregorian Strategy, but that pit is under stricter surveillance than the rest of the casino blackjack tables. Try to avoid any problems playing in Las Vegas. Remember, the casinos here do not even need a reason to prevent you from playing. If they see that you are winning too much or too often, even using the Gregorian Strategy, which does not involve card counting at all, you run the chance, *although small at least at this point,* of being barred.

The show is starting. I will write more later.

8:30 PM. The show is over and we are off to play blackjack for a little while. Remember, we are still on New York time, and although here in Las Vegas it is only 8:30 PM, our bodies and brains think that it is three hours later. We both are a little tired.

We are going to stroll around the blackjack pits together this time looking for a positively biased game, if we do find one, we are going to sit down to play for a while. The six-deck game here at the Nugget offers surrender and resplit Aces. Dealer hits soft 17.

11:00 PM. I just finished playing for about two hours and I took a beating. I lost $250 and I am done for the night. I am really tired. I asked the pit boss for a breakfast comp for two at the Carson street café in the lobby before I quit for the day. We are on our way up to the room now; I will recap the day up there.

Monday night. I won $87.50 at the Las Vegas club earlier, and I lost $250 here at the Golden Nugget tonight. Total play so far is four hours, and I am down $162.50 cash. This happens and that is just the way it is. Get used to it. Good night.

Day two. Tuesday. It is 9:00 AM and we are up, dressed, and ready to eat. I have that comp for the Carson Street café, and we are on our way.

There is a line to get in for breakfast, but if you have a comp—which we do—you get the VIP treatment and get to cut the line. Cool, huh?

9:45 AM. I ordered a mushroom and cheese omelet, and my girlfriend ordered a ham and cheese omelet. I also ordered a stack of pancakes for us to share, some toast, two large orange juices, and coffee, of course. When it is on them, *order it all* I always say; they can afford it. Comps actually cost the casinos nothing at all; it is an advertising tax write-off for them. Here in Las Vegas, comps are much easier to come by than in Atlantic City, and weekend room and holiday room comps are just as easy to get as regular during-the-week room comps. Also, meal comps are easier to get. There is more competition among the casinos for your business because there are so many more casinos here in Las Vegas than in Atlantic City.

10:45 AM. That was good! We are going to get in the car and cruise uptown to Caesars Palace Las Vegas. My lovely girlfriend wants to hit the forum shops there, so that will give me some time at the blackjack tables. It works out nicely, don't you think?

Noon. We are pulling up to Caesars. This is an impressive

place. We will valet-park the car and off we will go. We split up now for a while, planning to meet right here at the entrance in three hours, 3:00 PM. I am sitting at a slot machine just inside the main entrance. I am going to walk into the main casino and check out the games before I play.

12:30 PM. I am inside the main casino now, and it is amazing. The Caesars in Atlantic City pales in comparison to this place. Let's go play some casino blackjack. The game we will play is a six-deck with all the common Atlantic City rules, but here you have surrender and resplit Aces.

2:45 PM. I just finished playing for about two hours at a $25-minimum table sitting at third base with two other players. I picked up $187.50. I am in the green again; remember, I was down $162.50 from my loss at the Golden Nugget last night. I have to run and cash in my chips because I have to meet up with my girlfriend in fifteen minutes.

3:00 PM. Where is she? She is always late. That is all right, though, she has other good qualities. It is absolutely beautiful out! I think that we will go over to the Bellagio for a while—shopping for her and blackjack for me, so it works out well once again. Here she is!

4:00 PM. I am in the casino at the Bellagio, she liked my idea about coming over here for a while. She only bought a pair of pants and a shirt in the three hours she shopped. In three hours, the average guy could probably buy an entire wardrobe; I know I could. We will meet up at 6:30 PM for dinner; I am hungry now, actually. What else is new.

I am going to walk over to the back blackjack pit near the conservatory; it is usually not crowded there. The game offered here at this pit is a six-deck game with all the rules I like.

6:15 PM. Two hours of play, $25 minimum, and I won $137.50. *I will take it.* Since my play in Atlantic City last week, I have not had any really big wins—*or losses*, for that matter—so I guess I should be thankful. I have to go and cash in these chips; I also got a comp for a dinner buffet that happens to be very good. I have eaten there many times.

6:40 PM. Now it is my turn to be late. There was a line at the cashier's cage and I had to walk across the whole casino to meet up with my girlfriend at the entrance to the casino where the shops are. We are off to the buffet now.

7:15 PM. Another line at the buffet that we got to cut due to the comp. We are (okay, I am) sitting at the table at the buffet; she went for a food run. I am going to join her.

8:30 PM. We are just leaving the buffet now. We ate everything and then some! I feel like I am going to explode. We are going to go outside in front of the Bellagio and watch the beautiful dancing water fountains.

8:55 PM. The water/fountain show should start at any moment. We are leaning on the beautiful stone gate that surrounds the front of the Bellagio, standing dead center. The weather is perfect, around seventy-five or eighty degrees I would guess. Here we go! They are playing "Big Spender"—I love this song! I am going to stop writing for a while and watch this.

9:15 PM. Wow! That show is the coolest thing. We are going to walk over to Caesars again to play some more blackjack for a while—together this time.

10:15 PM. We are in the casino now. She wanted to stop and play a "Jackpot Party" nickel slot machine, which we are in front of right now. In all honesty that game is kind of fun. I am going to leave her here for a while and meet up with her in an hour.

11:30 PM. In an hour of play I picked up $75. I was up $150 at one point, but I obviously did not leave the table soon enough; I have to learn to be more careful. We are going to leave Caesars and go back to the Golden Nugget.

12:15 AM. We are in the car—with the top down, of course—cruising downtown on Las Vegas Boulevard. What a beautiful night! And the Strip just looks stunning all lit up. You really have to check this place out if you have never been here. My girlfriend and I are both pretty tired, and we are going to hit the room for the night. I will recap this excursion when we get to the room.

1:30 AM. We are in the room now. All right, let's figure out what is happening so far. I have played a total of nine hours up to this point. I have won $237.50 cash. I received the comp for the Carson Street café breakfast here at the Golden Nugget, $24 plus the comp for the dinner buffet at the Bellagio, $27. That comes to $51 in comps. My hourly cash win rate at this point, playing $25 a hand, is about $26. That is about right. I would like to write some more, but, well, *you know.*

Day three. Wednesday. Good morning! It is 9:30 AM. I called the casino host to see if I could get a comp to the breakfast buffet for two—of course I got it. We are going down there now.

10:15 AM. We had a little delay leaving the room because she, *my lovely companion,* was not actually finished with her makeup. Doesn't she realize how hungry a guy can get? Well, we are here at the buffet now. My comp was left with the buffet cashier so, again, we did not have to wait, we are VIPs! Yeah, right . . .

11:30 AM. What now? We finished the buffet, and we are both stuffed. I would like to take a nice leisurely stroll down to the Main Street Station hotel-casino. We haven't been outside yet, but I am sure it is beautiful.

1:30 PM. We are in the Main Street Station casino now; we took a few detours to check out several of the vendors selling things along Fremont Street. She picked up another shirt and a silver ring; *you know I have to go along with this.* She wants to play one of those Jackpot Party nickel slot machine games again, which is just fine with me. I am off to hit the blackjack tables! We will meet in two hours.

3:45 PM. I just had a scorching run at the tables, my best since even before my Atlantic City excursion—$525 in two hours. I am happy now! I won hand after hand playing $25 each; I started winning as soon as I sat down. I sat at first base with one other person, playing against a two-deck game with all the good Las

Vegas rules. Yes, life is good again! We are now going to walk across the street, via walkway, to the California; there is an excellent homemade ice cream shop there on the second floor. Time for decadence.

5:00 PM. We are sitting just across from the ice cream shop at a little outdoor café-style table, eating our ice cream. I am eating two huge scoops of vanilla ice cream covered with marshmallow, hot fudge, peanut butter, and whipped cream; does that sound good to you? Why don't you stop reading for a while and get yourself one of these things, wherever you are? You only live once you know. I am going to pay for this in the form of a whopping bellyache later, of course, so think about that before you do the same. My sweetie is having a chocolate malted.

5:45 PM. Wow, am I full! We are leaving the ice cream place now. We are going to cut through the California to the back of the Las Vegas Club. We are on our way over to Fitzgerald's to watch the *Viva Las Vegas* show. It is free, it is located in the casino, and it features an Elvis impersonator. Pretty cool.

6:30 PM. We are at Fitzgerald's, where I know several of the dealers. I will ask each of them how his cards are running. The Elvis thing does not start until 8:00, so I will play blackjack for a little while. She does not want me to, though, ha, ha.

8:30 PM. She was right, I shouldn't have played. I lost $225. That's the breaks. Elvis is on now! I am going to watch this with her for a while.

9:30 PM. Enough of that. He was not that good, or maybe it is me who is in a lousy mood. Anyway, we are now at the Golden Nugget casino again. She wants to play her little game, that Jackpot Party thing, and I am going to hit the tables. She will find me at the blackjack tables whenever she is done.

11:45 PM. I played for two hours and picked up $100. I have had enough of blackjack for today. I am sitting at the back bar just behind the blackjack pit as I write this. I have no idea where she is; I have to go and find her.

12:15 AM. I found her playing another game, which we are

sitting in front of right now, called "Winning Bid." It is one of these video slot games. She is almost out of nickels and I am ready for bed. I will recap when we get to the room.

1:00 AM. We are in the room now. So where are we . . . fifteen hours of blackjack so far. Cash won is $637.50. Comps total is $64. My hourly cash win rate is now $42.50. This is over my theoretical win rate again. You know what that means—losses are on their way. Good night.

Day four. Thursday, 10:00 AM. We are leaving tonight on the red-eye back to Newark. We are ready to leave and get breakfast. I again called the casino host and asked him for a comp for the buffet. I also asked him for a room comp—not that we are staying over another night, but this way we do not have to check out this morning; and if we get tired later we can come up to the room and hang out before our flight. Our flight does not leave Las Vegas until 12:30 AM. I got both breakfast and room comped. I love this place!

10:30 AM. We are at the buffet. Again there was a line, but not for us! After breakfast here at the Golden Nugget, we are going to get in the car and go uptown to Paris and do some sightseeing, as well as play some blackjack, of course.

11:15 AM. Breakfast is down and we are off, this being our last day here in Vegas and the weather being perfect as usual. We are going to enjoy the moment.

Noon. We are in the car with the top down, again, cruising uptown for some more Las Vegas action! You know, I haven't driven this car at all since we have been here. And I actually cannot be in a moving car and write at the same time, as it makes me feel sick, so I will write more when we arrive at the Paris casino.

12:25 PM. We are just pulling up to the valet at the main entrance to Paris. This place is just breathtaking, *really*. The Paris Las Vegas hotel-casino is probably right up there with the Bellagio, which is right across the street, and the Venetian up the Strip a bit. All right, gotta go, I will write more in the casino.

1:00 PM. We are in the casino of Paris now and she, my beloved, wants to play her little slot machine games. I do not understand her sometimes; she simply does not want to learn how to play blackjack. I tell her all the time that she should learn the Gregorian Strategy and do what I do, but she would rather play slot machines. I just do not understand it. It is fine, though. I will leave her here and find a blackjack game to play. We will meet here at this slot machine in two hours.

3:15 PM. I just got back from the tables. After playing for two hours at a $25 table, I left with exactly the same money I bought in for. At least I did not lose, right? The game went up and down the whole time; I was up $50 at one point, and I should have quit then. She wants to stay here and continue playing her games. She actually won $250 playing that silly Jackpot Party machine! She is doing better than me today. We are going to meet at 5:30 PM, same place, same machine.

5:30 PM. I lost $175 in two hours of play and she still has some of the money that she won before, *but* I did get us a comp for the great dinner buffet here. If you come here, you have to try it. We are off to eat.

6:30 PM. We are seated at the buffet now. Let me tell you, if we did not have this comp, we would not have eaten here; the line is just ridiculous. Even with our comp, we had to wait fifteen minutes for a seat. Time for grub.

7:30 PM. We are stuffed, we ate a little of everything—that is what buffets are all about, right? I don't know, do you? Just kidding. We are on our way over to Bally's, which has a neat little shopping mall downstairs. She wants to check it out and buy some souvenirs. Can you believe it! Not only did we once live here, but also we have Las Vegas paraphernalia all over the house back in New York! I don't care if she wants more; I say let her have it. While she shops, I am going to hit the blackjack tables in the casino.

8:00 PM. I am sitting at the bar, which is in the casino here at Bally's. This will be my last hurrah here in Vegas before we leave. We are going to meet in the blackjack pit next to the theater in two hours. Sooner if she finishes earlier, but that would be a miracle.

10:00 PM. I played for almost two hours and won $37.50. That is equivalent to one blackjack at $25 a hand. At least I ended this on an upward note, just as in Atlantic City. We have to get out of here now; we still have to get back to the hotel, check out, return the car, and catch the 12:35 AM flight for home.

11:00 PM. Well, we are checked out and returning to the airport to catch our flight. We are cutting this close, and I hate to rush. I will write more on the plane, *if we make it*.

1:15 AM. We made it! Don't ask me how. We had to run like maniacs through McCarran Airport. We were lucky that the airport was not busy and there was no one waiting at the rent-a-car place. I was beginning to think that we were going to be spending a day or two longer in Las Vegas—actually, that would have been just fine with me. We got to the terminal just as they were finishing up boarding. I was really sweating it.

Let's recap this Vegas excursion. Total play was twenty-one hours. I won $500 even. Total in comps, including all the meals and the one room comp, was $173. My cash win rate per hour of play was approximately $24. This is slightly below what my theoretical win rate should be here in Las Vegas. If I count my comps with my cash, however, I made $673. And if I take that figure and divide that by total hours of play, it would make my total hourly win rate about $32. Actually you should always count your comps as part of your total winnings, as I have told you before a few times, since you would have had to spend that money anyway, right?

We are just about to take off. I can see the beautiful casinos all lit up on the Strip. I always get a little sad when I leave this place. I truly love it. *I will come back soon*. I am going to get some sleep. I hope you enjoyed this little trip as much as I did. I will write more when I get back to New York. Good night.

Postscript

I took a few days off from writing, and I am going to take a few days off from blackjack as well, maybe even the rest of the week. I really do enjoy playing the game, actually, but for me, it is a job. We all have to do something for money; I just happen to play blackjack for a living. I mostly enjoy the freedom of it all, not having to answer to anyone, working when I want, not working when I do not; it is all up to me.

So what did we learn from the Atlantic City and the Las Vegas experiences? My intention was to show you, "in action," what you can expect if you use the Gregorian Strategy and play it flawlessly. Sometimes you will be over your expected win rate and sometimes you will be below it. Sometimes you will win a session, and sometimes you will lose a session, with your wins prevailing over time. Over the long run is when the advantage of using the Gregorian Strategy will show itself. If you play blackjack just for fun, as I imagine that most of you do, your "long run" may take a while to present itself. It really depends on how much and how often you play. The more you play with any kind of an advantage, the greater your chances of winning will become (it works the same way for the casinos). You will have your wins, *sometimes many consecutive ones*, and you will have your losses, *also sometimes many consecutive ones*. Personally, my longest consecutive winning streak lasted twenty-three sessions! My longest consecutive losing streak was eleven sessions. I count a session as the time spent playing at one table, no matter how long that may be. In one day, it is possible for me to play several sessions if I am jumping from table to table or casino to casino. Some players I know count sessions on a per-day basis. It is up to you how you will do it. I mostly look at things relating to "the game" as on a full-time basis, because that is the way that I play.

My schedule varies from twenty to forty-plus hours a week; it just depends on how I feel at the moment. I play three or four days a week with varying hours. I am comfortable playing this way and I always try not to spend too much time in any one casino. *You remember why, right?* Tell me yes, lie to me. Always remember that no matter how nice the casino personnel are to you, *the powers-that-be don't want you winning more than you lose.*

I know that the development of the Gregorian Strategy for multiple deck blackjack is going to make waves in the multibillion-dollar casino gambling industry. Until this new and revolutionary strategy really catches on, there will be many opportunities for practitioners of it to make some serious money. I fear that the powers-that-be, *and the casinos*, may eventually kill the game by attempting to change the rules in an effort to make the game just another "game," with a fixed house edge. To do this, the casinos would have to change the rules pretty dramatically, and doing so, *I also believe*, they will keep most of the blackjack-playing public away from the game and out of the casinos altogether. Most people who play blackjack do so because they believe, or they have heard, that the game can in fact be beaten. This intriguing piece of information is what brings them to the tables. It is what attracted me to the game. If the casinos do alter the game in such a way as to truly make it unbeatable, they will lose about half of the general blackjack-playing public, no doubt about it. Blackjack has been and hopefully will always be a thinker's game, and if they take that element away, well, that will be the end of the game.

Writing this book for me has really been a labor of love, not just for the game of blackjack but also for you, the new students of the Gregorian Strategy. I love to teach—maybe I should have been a schoolteacher—but I am a blackjack player, and I am very happy to be able to pass this knowledge on to you. In the beginning, I never had any intentions of sharing this new knowledge with anyone but a select few. I really do not know what compelled me to put this all down on paper. Believe it or not, this book really started as a note I wrote to myself on a napkin while sitting at a blackjack table playing at the Orleans casino in Las Vegas. Truly, had it not been for those who really believed, this book might never have been available to you. There is a lot of important and valuable information written down here. If you are in fact a true student of the game, and of the Gregorian Strategy, this book will pay for itself many, *many* times over in the casinos.

♦ | 8 | ♣

Advanced Strategies

If you have been paying attention to the preceding pages of this book—and I really do hope that you have—then you would have noticed that I decided to leave this section for the absolute last.

Know this before you choose to study and gain knowledge of this "advanced strategies" section of the book: what you have been learning up until now, before you even read another word, is all you will ever need to know in order to effectively beat this game over the long run, without too many problems from casino personnel. What I am trying to say is that if, in fact, you have attentively read this book and learned the strategy herein, you now know everything you need to know to become a consistent winner at the game of blackjack and enjoy a full 1-percent long-term advantage over the house.

But for those of you who may have a small case of obsessive-compulsive disorder and really want to pinch every minute drop of advantage out of this game, I just may have for you what the doctor ordered.

Please let me say something here. This chapter almost did not make it into this book: as I said above, learning the Gregorian Strategy as outlined in the preceding pages is enough to beat the house. But if you are of the type who, like me, wants to be a little more involved with this game than the next guy—who may even be using the Gregorian Strategy—then read on.

If you have made it through this entire book, you may have noticed that at times I do have somewhat of an attitude problem. And yes, I am about to yell at you again. *Before you read another word,* you had better have learned the rest of this book well enough to recite it page for page! This is absolutely essential; otherwise some of the upcoming information may not make sense to you. So, are you with me on this one? Again, we shall see.

I am now going to contradict myself *a little bit* here with respect to what I have already told you about card counting. What you are about to learn is in fact a card-counting system, combined with a quite ingenious betting system, which, if executed correctly with the already exceptionally powerful Gregorian Strategy, can and will give you a long-term advantage over the house—as much as 3 percent!

Problem Number 1: if you play using the strategy you are about to learn, you will run an even additional risk of being barred from playing blackjack in the state of Nevada. But the good news is that if you play near Atlantic City, or where barring is unlawful, you will do just fine. The strategy you are about to learn—let's call it the "Gregorian Count Strategy," or GCS for short—does have some fail-safes built into it, as you will soon see.

Before we really begin, let's go over some of the basic theory on card counting and why, in theory, counting works—and it certainly does work. Now, let's discuss why.

If you read the preceding pages of this book, you came across the segment that addresses card counting, its subsequent applications, and its consequent pitfalls, which mainly come from the common betting strategies associated with card counting in order to exploit your advantage at a particular moment. Card counting is in reality "card tracking." You are not "counting" the cards; you are tracking them, and thus the subsequent composition of the remaining deck, in order to see who has the advantage at that particular moment in time—you, or the dealer. This is very important, so pay attention. If you knew that the deck will be in favor of you winning the next few hands, you would bet more; if you knew that the deck will be in favor of the house or dealer winning the next few hands, you would bet less or not at all. This is the essence of card counting: you bet more when you have the advantage, and you bet less when the house or dealer does.

Let's look for a moment at a standard deck of cards. There are fifty-two of them, with four suits of each card numbered 2, 3, 4, 5, 6, 7, 8, 9, 10, jack, queen, king, and ace. We also know at this point that the suits are irrelevant, since a 2 is a 2 is a 2 is a 2. Got me?

All right, put your thinking cap on again and make sure that it is plugged in. We know that the average winning hand is 18.5, yes 18.5. I discussed this before, so there is no reason to go over it again. Trust me, the average winning hand is 18.5. Why am I telling you this now? Well, I am glad you asked—see, your thinking cap is working.

So let's think about it for a moment. If you knew that there was a disproportionate number of high cards left in the deck, then your chances of getting a good starting total (say, 18.5 or above) would go up, and you would then hold an advantage over the house, wouldn't you? Also, your chances of getting a blackjack would go up, and thus you would gain the higher payoff. Now, according to the old card-counting method, in order to exploit your advantage at this point—with a high count (a disproportionate number of high cards left in the deck)—you would have to raise your bet. This raising of the bet is a no-no, because the dealer or the pit boss just may be watching you at this moment, and he may think you are "counting cards," and you are!

So what will the house or dealer do at this point? Well, essentially they will have two choices. First, if you are playing in an area where barring is allowed, they *may* ask you to leave the casino, or "bar you." The second choice they have is to shuffle up on you—and this happens a lot, especially with two-deck hand-held games. If the dealer does shuffle up on you, he is essentially and effectively erasing your gained advantage. So what do you do at that particular point? You already have your bigger bet out on the betting area; you raised your bet, and that is why the dealer decided to shuffle up. Now *you* have a choice: do you just leave your bigger bet out there and take your chances with the next hand? Or do you take your bigger bet back off the betting area while the dealer shuffles, which is a dead giveaway that you are in fact counting cards?

You might say to me, "If I cannot raise my bet to exploit my advantage, what can I do?" Ah yes! What can you do? Good question! Well, I will tell you this: at this point, your first bet—that is, the first bet you place when you sit down to play blackjack—would be your largest. Does that make any sense to you? Think about it for a moment. Yes, you read it correctly, you will never raise your bet, never, ever. *How you will gain your additional advantage using the GCS is that you will bet less in low counts, when the deck is favoring the house.* Do you follow me? Let's try this another way. No matter how high the count goes, you will never raise your bet. Only when the count goes below a specific point will you then *lower* your bet a specific amount. Why? Let's say that the count goes low and you lower your bet. What can the house do to you? If they shuffle up on you, they will only be helping you, because by shuffling, the dealer will then bring the "count" back to a neutral point, and by the nature of using the Gregorian Strategy alone you will have regained your advantage!

This is cool stuff. Really think about it. The house cannot in any way hurt you by shuffling up on you; if you play this way, they can only help you by shuffling. This is basically the betting system that we will employ. With neutral or high counts, you will bet whatever amount your bankroll can support (see Chapter Five, on money management). With low counts, you will cut that bet by half. For example, let's say your basic bet is ten dollars. If the count goes low, you will bet five dollars, pure and simple. You can also do this with units or chips. Two chips or units in neutral or high counts and one chip in low counts—whatever works for you.

Now, this is when this whole thing gets a little more complicated. How will you actually track the cards? There are many ways to do this, some very simple and some very complex. The count we will use is somewhere in the middle. I am choosing this particular count for its effectiveness; also, once you begin to become familiar with it, in casino play you will actually find it easier to keep track of the cards more accurately and more quickly by learning to count the cards in groups, because they will cancel themselves out against each other. I know that this all sounds a little confusing to you at this point, but just stay with me on this for a while and it will all come together for you.

Each card will be assigned a particular numeric value—except the 8. We will not count the 8. The 8 will be valued at zero. The 2, 3, 4, 5, 6, and 7 are all valued at $+1$. For example, the dealer begins to deal, and his first three cards are a 5, 2, and 7. Your count would now be 3. Now, same scenario, but the dealer also deals a fourth card, an 8. What is your count? It is still 3. Remember, I said that we will not count the 8; 8 = zero. The reason why we do not count the 8 is that for our card-counting purposes, the 8 really acts as a neutral card. Now the 9, 10, jack, queen, king, and ace will all be valued at -1 (minus one). Let's say the dealer begins to deal again; the first three cards are ace, 10, and queen. What is your count? Your count would be -3, or down three. It has been my experience that if you are tracking the cards, it is easier to say "down" than "minus," but if minus works for you than just say minus.

All right, so essentially we have two groups of cards to worry about. The 2, 3, 4, 5, 6, and 7 are all in our $(+)$ group, and the 9, 10, jack, queen, king, and ace are all in our $(-)$ group. Remember, we will not count the 8. Let's try another scenario. You sit down to play with another player at the table. He is sitting in front of you, which means he gets his cards first. Now the dealer begins to deal. The dealer deals him a 9 and you an ace; the dealer's up card is a 4. The dealer then deals out an 8 to the guy in front of you and follows you up with a 2. What is your count? Your count is now zero. Let's add this up. The other player's 9 = −1, your ace = −1, the dealer's 4 = +1, the 8 = zero, and the 2 = +1. If you do the math, you will come up with zero. Are you following this? If not, go over it again until you do.

Now, what I want you to do is take a standard deck of cards, shuffle it, and practice "counting" the cards. If you do this correctly, you should begin your count at zero, and end up with a count of zero when the last card is dealt. Practice this over and over again until you can do it with no mistakes. It will take some time before you can "count" quickly, but learning to do this rapidly and accurately is very important. In reality, you should be able (in time, of course) to count down the whole deck in no more than twenty-five seconds, because in the casino under fire, the dealer will not wait for you to finish what you are doing; trust me on this one. The good news is that since all multiple deck blackjack games are dealt as "up" games—that is, all the cards are in fact dealt out to the players faceup—it will be easy for you to see everyone's cards so you can track them.

Now, most two-deck blackjack games are still dealt as "down" games, so you will have to wait until the players are done playing out their hands before you will be able to count all their cards. This is when you must be able to do so rapidly. It can be done more quickly if you learn to have the cards cancel themselves out against each other or count them in groups, as I have stated earlier. Here is how this works. If you notice that the guy next to you is dealt a 7 and a 10, these cards (one being +, the 7; the other being −, the 10) just cancel each other out. This is the trick to learning to count quickly, and another reason why I chose to have you learn this count. Basically, you are counting all the cards except the 8, so this "canceling effect" is very effective when quick accurate counting matters.

So, you are now a card counter, are you? Well, you now know

how to do it—that is, keep a count—but you still have some more work to do, buddy.

Just a word of advice here from one who knows. If you are really going to be a card counter, you must try to sit at the first-base or third-base position. The reason is this: you will not have to move your head while you are scanning over the table at the other players' cards. If you get really good at this, you will not even move your eyes, just use your peripheral vision. If you do have to move your eyes, it may not be a bad idea to get yourself a baseball cap, as the visor will prevent the casino pit personnel from seeing you move your eyes. Do not sit at the middle of the table if you are going to count cards! You will constantly be moving your head back and forth, attempting to see the other players' cards, and you will get nailed doing this. Am I making myself clear?

Some more good news. What you have been learning to do is keep a running count, and that is all the count you need to keep. In the old days, if you were keeping a running count, you would have had to convert that count to a true count for betting purposes, but we are going to be using a very simple and deadly-effective betting system. There will be no need to do any more conversions.

Are you with me so far? Let's go over this a bit more. If you have a high or "positive count," that would mean there is a disproportionate number of high cards left in the deck, and as such your chances of getting a high starting total or a blackjack would go up. In high counts, that high card you were hoping to catch on your splits and double downs will now be easier, or more likely to appear—good to know, don't you think? You just gained an additional advantage over the house.

Now, if the count were low or negative, there is a disproportionate number of low cards in the deck; and subsequently, your chances of getting a poor starting total would go up and your chances of catching that high card on your splits and double downs would drop—and you would lose some of your advantage.

If there were a high-count situation, then the dealer's chances of busting his stiff up cards would also go up, thus adding to your advantage. Subsequently, if there were more low cards left in the deck, a low-count situation, the dealer's chances of making a hand instead of busting would then go up, which is not good. This works the same for you, however, and there will be times when you will now have to modify your Gregorian Strategy according to your count in order to fully exploit your advantage. We will go over the specifics of this later on, so pay attention. I told you that this was going to be a little more complicated, but you just do not listen to me.

This altering of strategy, as you will soon learn, may work out to help you out in other ways though, so read on. You see, if you do alter your playing strategy from time to time, according to your count, it will look to others, namely to the dealer and pit boss, like you simply do not know how to play, as you will not be doing the same thing over and over again. It will look as if you just play by how you feel at the moment. This is exactly what you want. You want the powers-that-be to think of you as just a stupid blackjack player who will eventually lose it all! But I am getting ahead of myself here. Down the line a bit, you are going to learn how to alter your playing strategy according to the count. But for now, let's learn how you will use your count for betting purposes, which is even more important than altering your playing strategy. This "using the count" to alter your bet is actually quite simple and effective. That is just how I like things, uncomplicated—how about you? How you will use your count in order to bet actually depends on how many decks are in play. You can find this out two ways. The first is to simply ask the dealer; it is a reasonable question. The second is to look and see if the dealer is holding the cards. If he is holding them, it is either a one- or two-deck game. I am sure that you can tell the difference by just looking at the size of the pack the dealer is holding. If you happen to be walking up to this particular game, with the dealer holding the cards, and it happens to be toward the end just before the shuffle, take a look at the discard tray. I am sure you will be able to tell if it is more that one deck.

Now, if this is a shoe game, it may not be as easy to tell how many decks are in actual play. Sometimes four decks looks like six decks, and sometimes six decks looks like eight. After you do this for a while, you will be able to tell either by looking at the discard tray, or looking into the shoe. But in the beginning you may have to just ask.

Basically this is how it works—and it is very simple.

- If you are playing against a two-deck game, when the count goes below − 4 (down 4), you will lower your bet by half.
- If you are playing a four-deck game, when the count goes below − 6 (down 6), you will lower your bet by half.
- If you are playing a six- or eight-deck game, when the count goes below − 8 (down 8), you will lower your bet by half.

There is a little memorization involved here, but not much. I think you can handle it.

The betting system that we have just learned is very effective and simple enough, don't you think? By betting this way alone, even without altering your playing strategy, you will gain an even more significant advantage over the house using the Gregorian Strategy.

But this is when this whole thing becomes a bit more complex. This is the point where you will learn how to alter your playing strategy according to your count or running count. This is another time when it will be important for you to know how many decks are being used in play. The more cards in play, obviously the harder it will be to catch any one particular card—as you already know, because you did read the rest of this book, and you did come across the part where I discussed this in more detail, right?

Also, and to your advantage while using the Gregorian Strategy, the more decks in play, the flatter the decks will run with regard to the count. What I mean is, the more decks in play, the less dramatic the swings in the count will be, and the less you will have to worry about altering your playing strategy. You see, this is yet another of those times when the Gregorian Strategy itself actually uses the casino's own game, which they, the powers-that-be, have attempted to use against the average player (who is still using the old basic strategy) and gain an even greater advantage over him by increasing the number of decks in play. But instead, by using the Gregorian Strategy, you the player get to turn the tables once again and use the casino's own game against the house.

The main reason the casinos have switched over to multiple deck games (as I have discussed before) is to give them an even greater advantage, over the average player who is still using the old basic strategy, and over card counters using the old counting betting strategies. You see, a card counter who is still using the old basic strategy and an old counting system—which requires him to significantly raise his bet in high counts, and significantly lower his bet in low counts—needs to play against games with fewer decks. The reason is that there will be greater swings in the count, and a counter using the old ways needs dramatic swings in the count in order to exploit his advantage. None of this matters anymore when you are using the GCS; we are state-of-the-art now, baby! Tell me, can you dig it?

All right, let's really work on truly honing our blackjack skills to a razor-sharp point! Don't you just love this game? There are just so many possibilities. I really do get excited thinking about it, and I am glad to share this stuff with you. You know, believe it or not, even though I may at times seem a little—I don't know, nasty I guess—I really do like you.

If you are going to learn how and when to alter your playing strategy according to your count, either you had better know the Gregorian Strategy cold, or maybe I will just put another strategy chart here so you can refer back to it. Does that sound good to you? I don't care what you say, I am going to do it anyway, tough guy!

Here is another Gregorian Strategy chart and its key. You will need to refer back to this chart from time to time as we begin our discussion of how to alter your playing strategy according to your running count.

Before I begin with this segment, let me say this. If you simply use the Gregorian Strategy as outlined, using the count I have already taught you combined with the betting system I have also already taught you, believe me, you are already among the elite. You will now easily be able to beat this game and beat it badly without altering your playing strategy one bit. But if that obsessive-compulsive disorder is kicking in again, sit back, regroup, and let's proceed.

With a two-deck game, you will sometimes see dramatic swings in the count, and this is the game that you will be altering your strategy the most playing against. That also means that you will be changing your bet the most often.

Just for your information, the one- and two-deck games are under the most scrutiny from the pit and also the eye in the sky. Honestly, you may just want to avoid two-deck games and stick with the shoe games, which the powers-that-be are more lax about with their eyeballs, if you get my meaning. Me, I like two-deck games because I like to hold the cards, plus I can count at the speed of light at this point in my life while at the same time playing out my hands, betting correctly, and even carrying on a conversation with a couple of people. Soon, if you practice and play under fire for a while, you will be able to do the same thing. You will see!

Two-Deck Games

You already know that if you are playing against a two-deck game, and the count goes below −4, you will drop your bet by

DEALER HAS

YOU HAVE	2	3	4	5	6	7	8	9	10	A
5–8	H	H	H	H	H	H	H	H	H	H
9	DD	DD	DD	DD	DD	DD	H	H	H	H
10	DD	DD	DD	DD	DD	DD	DD	DD	H	H
11	DD	DD	DD	DD	DD	DD	DD	DD	H	H
12, 13	H	H	H	H	H	H	H	H	H	H
14	H	H	S	S	S	H	H	H	H	H
15	H	S	S	S	S	H	H	H, SR	H, SR	H, SR
16	S	S	S	S	S	H	H, SR	H, SR	H, SR	H, SR
17–21	S	S	S	S	S	S	S	S	S	S
A/2 or A/3	H	H	H	DD	DD	H	H	H	H	H
A/4 or A/5	H	H	DD	DD	DD	H	H	H	H	H
A/6	H	DD	DD	DD	DD	H		H H	H	H
A/7	H	DD	DD	DD	DD	S	S	H	H	H
A/8 or A/9	S	S	S	S	S	S	S	S	S	S
2/2 or 3/3	H	H	SP	SP	SP	H	H	H	H	H
4/4	H	H	SP	SP	SP	H	H	H	H	H
5/5	DD	DD	DD	DD	DD	DD	DD	DD	H	H
6/6	H	H	SP	SP	SP	H	H	H	H	H
7/7	SP	SP	SP	SP	SP	SP	H	H	H	H
8/8	SP	SP	SP	SP	SP	SP	SP	H, SR	H, SR	H, SR
9/9	SP	SP	SP	SP	SP	S	SP	SP	S	S
10/10	S	S	S	S	S	S	S	S	S	S
A/A	SP	SP	SP	SP	SP	SP	SP	SP	H	H

KEY: H = Hit DD = Double Down S = Stand SP = Split SR = Surrender half. You remember that much, right? Well, also at the down 4 count, you will not double down your two-card total of 9 versus the 2, or your two-card total of 9 versus the 3. Instead, you will hit. The reason for this is, as you already know, the dealer often makes strong end totals with the 2, and often the 3, especially with low counts. With fewer high cards left in the deck, the dealer is even less apt to bust with either of these up cards, and more apt to make a strong hand. So you will not double down the 9 against the dealer's 2 or 3 and risk losing twice the money when the count goes to down 4 or lower. Instead, hit. Also, do not split your 9s versus the 2 if the count goes below -4, and do not split your 9s against the 3 if the count goes below -5. Instead, stand. If the count does goes below -5, do not split your aces against the 2. Instead, hit them, and play them out as outlined in the Gregorian Strategy chart.

If you are playing against a two-deck game and the count goes to $+4$ or above, do not hit your hard 15 versus the dealer's 2, or your hard 14 versus the dealer's 3. Instead, stand. If the count goes to $+6$ or above while playing against the two-deck game, split your 9s against the dealer's 7. You will then have a chance at having twice the money on the table when you hold a definite advantage!

I am going to hate myself for saying this, but if while you are playing against a two-deck game, the count goes above $+8$, raise your basic bet by half. At this point, you really are favored to win, and the temptation is just too hard to resist! That is just about it for a two-deck game. Again, simple and smart.

Four-Deck Games

You already know that with a count of -6 or below, you will cut your basic bet in half when playing against a four-deck game, right? Also, at a count of down 6 or below, you will not double down your two-card total of 9 versus the dealer's up cards of 2 or 3. Instead, you will hit it. Remember, the dealer can and often will make a strong hand with either a 2 or a 3 as his up card, especially with low counts, because of the disproportionate number of low cards left in the deck. Also, you will not split your 9s versus the dealer's up cards of 2 or 3 if the count falls below down 6. Instead, you will stand. You will also stand with a soft 18, ace/ 7, with a count of down 6 versus the dealer's 2, and you will not double down the soft 18 versus the dealer's 3. Instead, you will also stand. You do not want to risk any more money when the dealer's chances of making a hand go up. At a count of down 7, in a four-deck game, do not split your aces versus the dealer's 2. Instead, hit them.

If the count goes above 6 in a four-deck game, do not hit you hard 15 versus the dealer's 2 or your hard 14 versus the dealer's 3. Instead, stand. Also, with a count of + 6 or above, you will now split your 9s versus the dealer's up card of 7.

Six- and Eight-Deck Games

As I have said earlier in this chapter, the more decks involved in play, the more flat the count will run as the game is played out. Most multiple deck games that the casinos offer to us these days consist of six or eight decks. All the casinos of Atlantic City use either six or eight decks. For the most part, you will notice as you actually begin to play against games with six or eight decks that the needs to modify your strategy according to the count will often be few and far between. That really works out very well for us using the Gregorian Strategy; the less work, the better, I always say! But there will be those times when you will have to alter your playing strategy. We will go over that now.

You already know that you drop your basic bet by half if the count falls below down 8 in a six- or eight-deck game. At a count of down 8, with either the six- or eight-deck game, you will not double down your two-card total of 9 against the 2 or 3. Instead, you will hit. You also will not split your 9s versus the dealer's up card of 2 or 3. Instead, you will stand. You will now also stand with a soft 18 versus the dealer's up card of 2, and you will not double down your soft 18 versus the dealer's up card of 3, with a count of down 8 or below; your chances of winning against either of the aforementioned dealer up cards is substantially reduced. Down 8 or below in a six- or eight-deck game, do not split your aces against the dealer's up card of 2, either. Instead, hit them. If the count goes above 8, do not hit your hard 15 versus the dealer's up card of 2, and do not hit your hard 14 against the dealer's up card of 3. Instead, stand. Now with this high count, +8 or above, you will split your 9s against the dealer's up card of 7.

You will also notice during this advanced strategies section, I have not mentioned anything to do with the cut card. In the old days, using the old counting techniques and betting strategies, where the cut card was placed was very important. But using the GCS, this simply does not matter at all.

Just a few more words. Today, many casinos are preventing players from entering the game once the dealer has begun to deal out to the players. This is known as "no midshoe entry." This practice was instituted to prevent people from back-counting, or "Wonging." When an individual uses either of these practices, what he is in fact doing is observing the dealer—right from the beginning of the shoe or decks—deal out the cards and counting the cards as they are dealt *before* he sits down to play, in an attempt to find a positive count. Actually, I do this often along with looking for a positively biased table. Now, I know that you know what a biased table is—don't you? Doing this, back-counting or Wonging, gives you an even greater advantage over the house. With a "no midshoe entry" game, however, you will be unable to do this sort of thing.

Well, that just about does it for the recommended changes to your Gregorian Strategy with regard to the count. It really is not very complicated, and you will see as time progresses, and you continue to play the game, that all of this will become like second nature to you—almost an automatic reflex or conditioned response.

Really, even more important than learning to modify your strategy according to the count is learning the Gregorian Strategy without any modifications at all, and learning to use the count so you can make use of the betting strategy that you learned earlier. Learning the Gregorian Strategy along with my betting system will make you all but unbeatable at the blackjack tables. Believe that!

If you have learned how to count so that you can use my betting strategy, you are well ahead of the game already, and if you have in fact learned how to modify your strategy according to your count, you really are the best of the best. You can rest assured that if you have learned from this book and gotten to this point successfully, you really are now one of the elite; there are very few people on this planet who will be able to outplay you. Except me, of course! Well, I certainly do wish you the best of luck, and who knows? Maybe someday we will be sitting next to each other at the tables somewhere.

Conclusion

Well, there you have it. The Gregorian Strategy took three years of research and development, two years of theory, and one year of proving that the theory works. And work it does! What this new knowledge will do to the game, I do not know. But it will be interesting to see.

If they—and you know who "they" are by now—do come up with some new twist in an attempt to make the game, let's say, a little more challenging, I say bring it on! I am more than ready. This is a strange and rewarding profession you and I have chosen. For me, it is not really the money at all, it is just a hell of a lot of fun!

Important note: The preceding pages of this book contain some very valuable information. You now can benefit from my past mistakes and profit from my successes without having to spend years in the casino and gambling environment. I truly hope that you take the information in this book and use it to benefit yourself and your lifestyle. The glitz and glamour of the casinos are indeed hard to resist.

Some people, however, have no control over their actions in the gambling arenas. There is a big, dark downside to every good thing, and there is also no way around it. I do not think that this book would be truly complete without talking about that dark side. For many, the addiction to casino gambling is a downward spiral into a pit of emotional and financial despair. As I have said many times in this book, the casinos do not care who you are or what your situation is; they just want your money, all of it, as fast as they can get it. Keep this in mind because no one is immune to the draw of the excitement that is so abundantly available in the casino environment or in gambling itself.

For myself, the only game I play in the casino is blackjack. I am not a gambler at all—I truly consider myself an investor in the game. The sole reason I even play blackjack is because I can beat the game in the literal sense. Now you can, too, if you really want it badly enough. Study this book, learn the Gregorian Strategy, acquire discipline, apply the money management skills, stick to my recommendations for bankroll and playing stakes, and you will do just fine!

Chapter-by-Chapter Summary

What I have decided to do in this section is take each chapter and summarize it for you as a quick reference guide. If you do go to the casinos, or on a trip to a casino-resort, bring this book along with you. If you have not played blackjack for a while after learning the Gregorian Strategy, you can use this summary section to brush up and sharpen your blackjack skills. I am attempting to do everything I can to make you the best blackjack player that you can possibly be, a true expert in the game. You also have to put in your time, and believe in yourself, to make it a reality. A winner is not born; a winner is made. If you were to look at the heads of corporations or government, actors, actresses, musicians, teachers, doctors, nurses, clergy—any successful people for that matter—what would they have in common? A strong desire to succeed! It is all about will and willingness to learn to become the best at something. The road to success is very narrow and traveled by only a few, while the road to failure is wide, and traveled by many. I want you to succeed.

INTRODUCTION

The introduction of this book discusses my beginnings as a blackjack player up to my career as a professional. It discusses "team play" in Atlantic City, which actually gave me the bankroll to play professional blackjack in the casinos of Las Vegas and Atlantic City today.

This section discusses the power and pitfalls of card counting, the weakness of old basic strategy, and the advent of the most powerful and best strategy ever developed for the game to date: the Gregorian Strategy.

The introduction also highlights the casinos of Las Vegas and gives strong recommendations as to which to play in and which to avoid.

Chapter One:
THE GAME TODAY

Chapter One discusses the fact that old basic strategy was never designed for blackjack games that contain multiple decks—the most commonly offered casino blackjack games today. In the introduction section of this book, you will find some more detail into the actual development of the Gregorian Strategy, addressing the shortcomings of using old basic strategy against multiple deck blackjack games.

Chapter One delves more deeply into the reasons why old basic strategy will not work, from a moneymaking standpoint, when played against multiple deck blackjack games; these reasons should be clearly understood. This chapter attempts to familiarize you with those reasons. Chapter One also discusses the fundamentals of card counting, including coverage of card counting's downfalls. It notes that most casinos are now in fact using very high-tech software to discover and subsequently bar proficient card counters. Chapter One also touches on the fact that there is still an element of organized crime present even in today's modern casinos. It covers the subject of progressive-betting systems and why none of them is a viable option when attempting to beat the game over the long term. Chapter One discusses probability theory and the Law of Large Numbers, both of which should be understood by anyone who is considering any type of casino gambling, not just blackjack. Chapter One goes on to discuss some of the advantages of using the Gregorian Strategy versus the old basic strategy, and this is covered in detail throughout this book. Importantly, this chapter emphasizes that just as the old basic strategy was not designed to be played against multiple deck games, the Gregorian Strategy is also not designed to be played against single deck games. Each strategy, the old basic strategy and the Gregorian Strategy, is designed for a very specific purpose. You must use the right tool for the job; you would not attempt to place a screw in a wall with a paper plate, would you?

Finally, Chapter One briefly discusses the development of the game and where it may be going in the future. The chapter goes on to describe in detail "the game," percentage wins and losses, and your advantage *over the house* using the Gregorian Strategy.

Chapter Two:
HOW TO PLAY THE GAME

Chapter Two tells you how to actually sit down and play the game, and how the house essentially sets up the game. Common terms used in the game, and common practices such as how the cards are dealt during the game, are also discussed. Chapter Two goes on to explain the differences between an "up game" and a "down game," and how you as a player will handle your cards and play out your hands in each. This chapter begins to touch on the rules of the game and their importance. The subject of "the rules" is of paramount importance and must be fully understood. This subject is addressed throughout the book and is crucial. This chapter discusses in detail how to use the rules of the game to your advantage and how to exploit them using the Gregorian Strategy. This chapter also describes the best places to play blackjack in Atlantic City and in Las Vegas.

Chapter Three:
THE GREGORIAN THEOREM

Chapter Three *must* be fully understood. This chapter discusses and illustrates the dealer's pat/bust potential in detail with respect to multiple deck games, and how and (more importantly) why you make very specific plays according to the Gregorian Strategy. Chapter Three goes on to explain and illustrate why the old basic strategy does not work, and will never work when used alone against multiple deck games. It delves deeply into how to play out your hands strictly according to the Gregorian Strategy. This chapter also contains the Gregorian Strategy chart. This chapter should be read and reread several times because of its importance. This chapter is the basis and the foundation of this book and as such, it must be fully understood by any new practitioner of the Gregorian Strategy.

Chapter Four:
PUTTING THE PLAN INTO ACTION

Chapter Four discusses the importance of practice and study. At this point in the book, you have the theory and the strategy, but in order to make it actually work, you must devote the time necessary to become a winner. This chapter begins to touch on the things that the casinos and the casino personnel can and will do in order to "help you lose." This chapter is designed to give you an idea of what you will come in contact with in the casino environment, and how to counteract the casinos' ploys to get your money, and instead get theirs. This chapter talks about casino barring—where it is (unfortunately) legal (Las Vegas) and where it is not (Atlantic City).

Chapter Five:
MONEY MANAGEMENT

Chapter Five is the chapter that will separate the "men from the boys," so to speak. This chapter discusses the typical serious player's demeanor and mindset. Very importantly, it discusses the money management techniques that are an integral part of becoming a winning player. Without proper money management skills, you are doomed to failure regardless of how well you may have learned the Gregorian Strategy. This chapter gives my strong recommendations on bankroll and playing stakes, which must be strictly adhered to. This chapter discusses linkage and the playing of multiple hands. It talks about the acquisition of discipline and its inherent importance. Chapter Five goes on to talk about casino and dealer cheating, a rare but real phenomenon that you must be aware of. This chapter also discusses the fact that you must "play out your hands like a machine" strictly according to the Gregorian Strategy. Never play hunches, and do not guess. Very importantly, this chapter discusses "biases," an exceedingly real part of the game. You must understand biases and how to make them work for you, instead of against you. Their importance is discussed in detail.

Chapter Six:
CASINO ETIQUETTE

Chapter Six discusses what is expected of you in regard to your behavior at the tables as a blackjack player. It also reiterates how the casino uses the game *itself* against the player as a psychological attack. This very real phenomenon is discussed in detail, and you are taught to be aware. Being aware is what will allow you to counteract the casinos' ploys. Chapter Six also discusses the importance of keeping a good relationship with the dealer and pit bosses by tipping the dealer at the appropriate times and amounts, and more importantly, for the right reasons. You are urged to pay close attention to the subject of tipping, because it is done for more than the obvious reasons. This chapter talks about socializing in the casino during play and getting rated during your play, which is very important. Also in Chapter Six, we learn about the dark side of the casino environment, and how to handle the casino personnel.

Appendix B

Dos and Don'ts

Don't play at crowded tables.
Don't play with a short bankroll.
Don't drink alcohol while you are playing.
Don't give advice to other players.
Do learn the Gregorian Strategy and play it perfectly.
Do seek out games offering you the best rules.
Do practice.
Do acquire discipline.
Do use proper money management skills.
Do secretly hide chips if you are winning.
Do tip the dealer when you are winning.
Do leave the table when you are getting heat.
Do read this book over and over again until you can practically recite it on your own!

Glossary

Action: to play

Anchor Seat: also known as third base, the seat to the dealer's extreme right

Bet: your wager

Blackjack: a hand that contains an ace and a 10-value card

Bust: to go over 21

Burn Card: the card taken from a newly shuffled deck and placed in the discard tray

Buy-in: the amount of money you convert into chips

Bankroll: the total amount of money you are willing to risk at gaming

Barring: being ejected from a casino

Comp: complimentary; a gift from the casino for your play

Cut Card: the card that is placed in the deck that determines when the dealer will shuffle

Card Counter: any person who keeps track of the cards as they are played

Double Down: when you ask for just one more card and double the bet

Dealing Down: when the cards are dealt face down

Dealer: the person who deals the cards and runs the game

Discard Tray: where the used cards are placed

Eye in the Sky: the camera above your head watching your every move

Gregorian Strategy: the ultimate strategy for multiple deck blackjack

Hit: to ask for another card

High Roller: a person who wagers a lot of money

Insurance: a side bet offered when a dealer has an ace showing

Push: a draw

Pat Hand: a total between 17 and 21

Pit Boss: a person who oversees the game and the dealers

Soft Hand: a hand that contains an ace

Shoe: a device from which the dealer pulls the cards

Stiff Hand: any total lower than 17

Shuffling Up: When the dealer stops the game and shuffles the cards to eliminate a card-counter's advantage

Toke: a tip

Up Game: when the cards are dealt face up